Collector's Guide to

# HOUSEKEEPING TOYS

1870 – 1970

from Metal to Plastic

*Identification and Values*

Margaret Wright

COLLECTOR BOOKS
A Division of Schroeder Publishing Co., Inc.

Cover design · Beth Summers Book design · Erica Weise
Cover photography · Charles R. Lynch

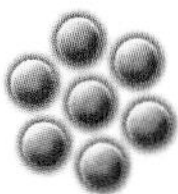

**COLLECTOR BOOKS**
P.O. Box 3009
Paducah, Kentucky 42002-3009

www.collectorbooks.com




The current values in this book should be used only as a guide. They are not intended to set prices, which vary from one section of the country to another. Auction prices as well as dealer prices vary greatly and are affected by condition as well as demand. Neither the author nor the publisher assumes responsibility for any losses that might be incurred as a result of consulting this guide.

*Searching for a Publisher?*

We are always looking for people knowledgeable within their fields. If you feel that there is a real need for a book on your collectible subject and have a large comprehensive collection, contact Collector Books.

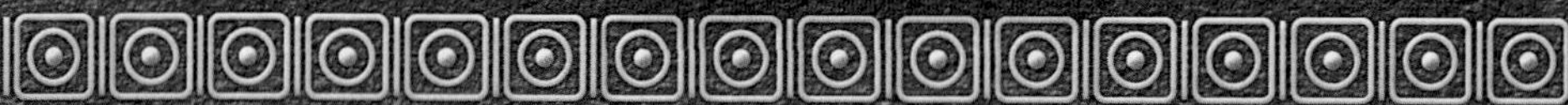

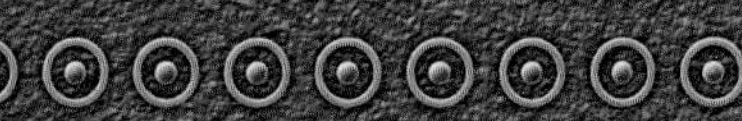

# Contents



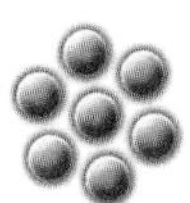

# Dedication

I dedicate this book to my family — Bonnie Celeste, Mark, Bonnie Poladian, Andrew, and Matthew, and in memory of my beloved "Petersburg Gus."

# Acknowledgments

Richard Chaisson, Athol town historian, Athol, Massachusetts, for information on N.D. Cass Co.

Paul A. Jones, Jr., of Jonesville, Michigan, for his generous information and help with his company, Kiddie Brush & Toy Co.

Booneville Library, Arkansas, for help with information on Wolverine Toy Company.

R. Brian Corbett, board president of Grosvenor House Museum, Jonesville, Michigan, for information and photos of the museum's collection of Kiddie Brush & Toy Co. toys.

Petersburg Public Library, Petersburg, Virginia, for assistance in collecting research materials.

# Introduction

This book about toy household furnishings "Made in USA" is an attempt to extend a broader view of dramatic contributions made by American toy companies, many mentioned only as footnotes in toy books. New material on companies like N.D. Cass, Kiddie Brush & Toy Co., Amsco, Gotham, and others will be featured. Many manufacturers must be considered to present the scope of our history embedded in these toys.

America is noted for its early efforts in advertising toys. Many toy cabinets, cupboards, refrigerators, cleaning sets, and other conveyors were provided with real national brand products to promote toy sales. This benefited both toy and commodity companies.

Most toy companies associated with production of trucks, autos, trains, horsedrawn vehicles, airplanes, cap pistols, etc. made housekeeping toys also. Arcade, Hubley, Kenton, J. & E. Stevens, A.C. Williams, Champion, Grey Iron, and Kilgore are just a few that found housekeeping toys important enough to manufacture.

This book tells the story of our country, our people. By observing Wolverine's refrigerator doors, we see what people ate. Prior to 1960, products shown on the door had very few bottles and jars. By 1960, bottles and jars, whether of glass or plastic, lined the shelves.

The toys in this study are historical documents. I have demonstrated that American history can be taught with 20 toys on a table, beginning with an 1880 cast-iron stove and ending with a plastic tea set, components of the Industrial Revolution and modern technology.

When I have the good fortune to purchase all childhood toys from one family, I consider having found a complete museum intact. Nothing has been added since childhood; the toys have been preserved; they are pure. I hope this study will serve as a museum guide to housekeeping toys, made in the USA, 1870 – 1970.

# PRICING

Pricing is so difficult because it is affected by so many variables. Prices differ from region to region. They are affected when a large collection is sold and gluts the market. They differ from small antique malls to large toy shows. Bids and sales on eBay further complicate prices.

Toys move in and out of favor; prices fluctuate, so I have tried to survey recent prices from private collectors, antique malls and shops, flea markets, and large toy shows.

Toys or sets in the text will fall into two categories. A lower price is given to toys in good condition with normal wear. The higher price is applied to those toys reaching excellent or near-mint status. The reader must determine where the toy fits on the scale.

Values given are meant only as a guide, as an indication of possible value; they are not intended to set prices.

# STOVES

### *The Evolution of the Cookstove*

Tracing cooking back to medieval times, it is evident that cooking and heating were done in fireplaces from the fourth century to the sixteenth century throughout Europe and England. Fireplace cooking was hard and required strength and alertness from the cook. Trammels and other devices helped with the burdensome maneuvering of heavy pots, but clothing could catch fire, spills could cause burns, and other serious accidents could occur. Out of necessity, man moved on. His discontent powered him to create a better way to cook.

From the 1600s to c. 1830, there were many attempts to create a better cooking machine. It was George Bodley, a British ironmaster, who, c. 1802, patented a closed top range with boiling holes that became the pattern for British and American stoves. By the mid-nineteenth century, the cast-iron kitchen range was moving into American homes across the nation. The toy range was not far behind.

The first toy stoves were like those in real kitchens. They were generally made by real stove manufacturers. Orr, Painter, & Co. of Reading Stove Works, Reading, Pennsylvania, advertised the Dainty in the 1889 Montgomery Ward catalog, and Ideal Mfg. Co. of Detroit, Michigan, offered Pet and Baby in the Marshall Field catalog in 1892.

When the toy cast-iron stove debuted in retail catalogs, all things were in place to guarantee success. By 1896, better postal rates enhanced catalog buying. Bulk rates and rural free delivery sent catalogs to remote areas. By the 1900s, retail catalog buying had created a solid undercurrent of consumerism. People were buying more of everything, including toys.

Little Fanny was made by Philadelphia Stove Works before 1900. It is in excellent condition, and has a black finish, cast-iron oven rack, and heavy tin chimney. The embossed designs add artful significance. 11¾"l, chimney 13"h. **$500.00 – 800.00.**

J. & E. Stevens of Cromwell, Connecticut, patented the Rival, July 30, 1895, as clearly noted on the back. It was advertised as "Rival toy range, with elevated warming oven and with kettles, spider, etc., is finely polished and nickel plated and is undoubtedly one of the handsomest toy ranges on the market," J. & E. Stevens, c. 1895. 14¼"h x 16"w x 8½"d. **$2,000.00 – 2,300.00.**

*Note: This Rival appears in the John Smythe catalog, 1917, with a right-side shelf added. The 1895 model weighed 28 pounds and cost $2.85 in 1903. The 1917 model, even adding a shelf, weighed 23 pounds and cost $3.25; less iron, higher cost.*

Baby, marked "Ideal Mfg'r. Co. Detroit Mich." c. 1890s. 9¼"h x 15½"w x 8¾"d. **$600.00 – 800.00.**

The Pet is described as "A perfect working toy range, has 4 boiling holes, reservoir, dumping grate, reservoir damper, etc."Kenton Toy Co. or Ideal Mfg. Co., c. 1890s. 12"h x 11"w x 6¼"d. **$350.00 – 450.00.**

Kenton's nickel-plated Royal is well-designed with warming ovens, ash shaker, damper, turning grate, and four opening doors. "Kenton Brand" is embossed on the back. Kenton Toy Co., c. 1915 – 1920. 12"h x 14¼"w x 6½"d. **$500.00 – 600.00.**

Featured is the mid-size range in the long line of Hubley's Eagle ranges. It is nickel-plated with original furnishings, as shown in Butler Brothers' 1921 catalog. Hubley Mfg., c. 1920. 6½"h x 7½"w x 3½"d. **$150.00 – 200.00.**

The tiny Star is also by Hubley, appearing in 1920 with no utensils. In 1925, utensils were added. It has nickeled highlights, tin sides and back, removable backpiece, and original utensils. Hubley Mfg. Co., c. 1920s. 4½"h x 3¾"w x 3"d. **$75.00 – 100.00.**

Clara is very ornate and attributed to J. & E. Stevens, c. 1915. Utensils are original with stove. 3½"h x 5½"w x 4"d. **$200.00 – 250.00.**

### *Cooking with Gas*

By 1840, when gas began to be used for cooking in England, the Industrial Revolution had long been in force. The gas age for cooking arrived in America in the 1890s but was not met with enthusiasm from consumers. Gas was very explosive and controls were not perfected until the early 1900s. Food was overcooked or undercooked; there were no adjusting devices. By 1920, better engineering resolved these problems, and gas was accepted in American kitchens.

It is easy to see why gas transformed the adult kitchen to one cleaner and more hygienic. Wood and coal created soot, ashes, and messy maintenance of fuel storage. Gas stoves simply hooked into the source with no fuss. Toymakers made haste to promote this up-to-date change, and toy gas stoves, all sizes, styles, and colors, poured into the marketplace. Companies like Kenton, Hubley, Arcade, and many others produced faux burners because gas was so explosive and could be very dangerous in the hands of children. Tappan Stove Company in the 1930s produced a toy working gas range with real gas connections. This was a miniature version of the full-size range. Retail stores and catalog houses shied away from this "real" gas range.

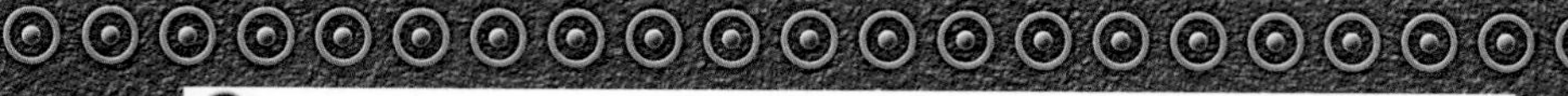



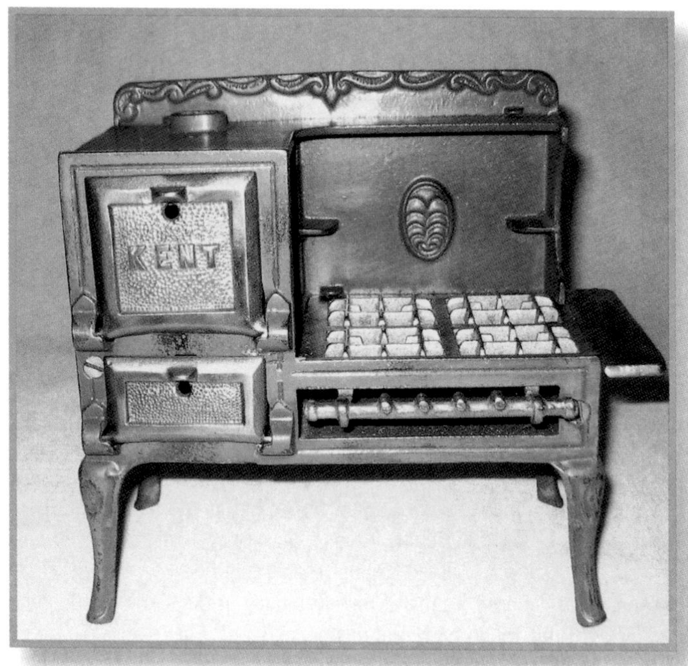


The Kent has original paint, four burners, two warming shelves, and two ovens. It has nickeled highlights. Kenton Toy Co., c. 1927. 6¾"h x 8"w x 3½"d. **$125.00 – 175.00**.

The Eagle is in mint condition. Hubley produced at least five different sizes of this model from 11½" to 4¾". Hubley Mfg. Co., c. 1920s. 4¼"h x 4¾"w x 2¼"d. **$75.00 – 100.00.**

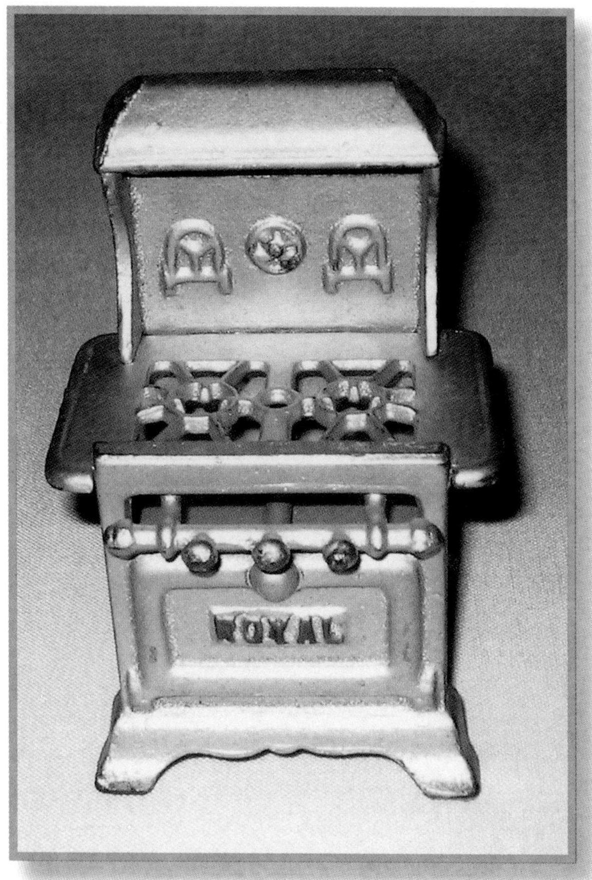


The Royal began to appear in the 1920s. It copies the adult Auxiliary model. Usually silvered, with one or two burners, they were dimestore stock, inexpensive, and sold by the hundreds. A. C. Williams, c. 1920 – 1930s. 4¼"h x 3"w x 2½"d. **$25.00 – 45.00.**

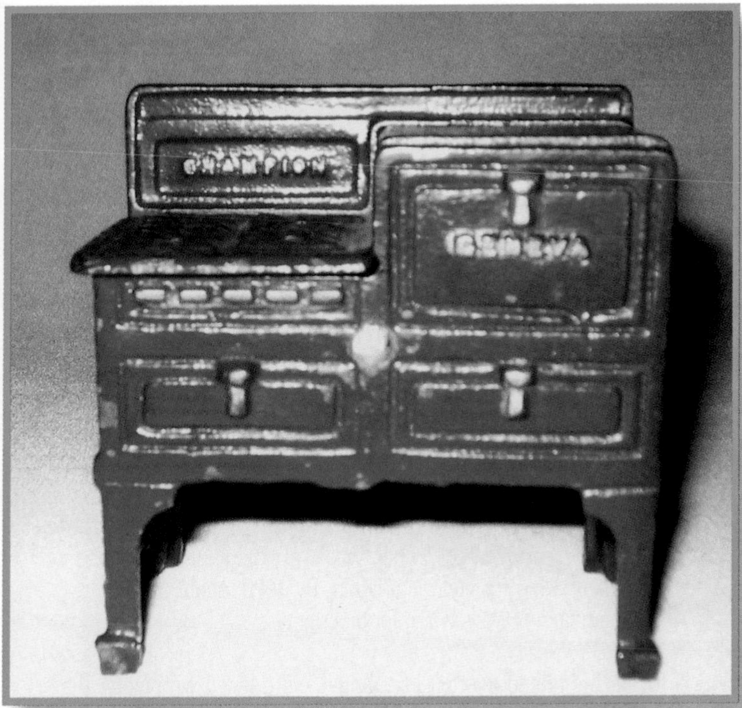

Two sizes of Champion stoves were issued, an upright Daisy and the Geneva. Champion Hardware Co., c. 1930. 3"h x 3¼"w x 2½"d. **$50.00 – 75.00**.

### *Hidden Fire – Electricity*

There is a direct change in the application of fuels in the electric range. The cast-iron stoves are reminiscent of early man's cooking with direct fire; with the electric range, the flame has become heated wires, representing a technological change.

In the late nineteenth century, gas was losing preference as electricity was gaining. Thomas Edison's light bulb (1889) was replacing gas lamps, and, by 1907, competition between two major energy sources was evident. Gas fixtures were stationary. Electrical outlets allowed fixtures to be portable. Electricity needed no ventilation and caused no unpleasant residue, but much of the public was wary, beginning slowly with only wiring for electrical lights. By 1920, about 34% of American homes were wired for electricity.

Toymakers tooled for cast-iron ranges were faced with many difficulties in a transition to lighter metals required in electric stoves. These ranges would not be involved with direct flame and cast-iron was not needed. Until World War II, many companies continued to produce toy cast-iron stoves, but change was inevitable. The lighter weight and cleaner aspects of the toy electric range appealed to parents and children.

The label on the Elektro states: "Elektro-Electric Toy Range, Manufactured by D.C. Hughes & Co., Chicago. No. 4486." In 1916, the company's catalog of real ranges featured this toy model. It is identical to the full-size range. D.C. Hughes & Co., 1916. 16½"h x 10½"w x 6"d. **$175.00 – 200.00**.

The Empire range, made by Metal Ware Corp., was produced in different sizes and colors for decades. The large green range carries a label: "Pat. June 17th, 1924." It has off and on switches and a metal oven rack. Metal Ware Corp., 1924. 17"h x 21"w x 8½"d. **$500.00 – 600.00.**

Empire blue range has one switch to control burners and one switch to control the twin ovens. Metal Ware Corp., c. 1930. 15"h x 15½"w x 6"d. **$600.00 – 800.00**.

The Little Lady with red accents has a paper label picturing a clock and the name, "Little Lady." A special feature is the glass window in the oven door. Metal Ware Corp., 1950. 11"h x 12"w x 6"d. **$65.00 – 95.00**.

Little Chef was produced by Ohio Art Company after the company purchased Tacoma Metal Products in 1955. It appeared in the Ohio Art catalog, 1956, declaring: "This is the finest range combination ever made." The window in the oven door was special at the time. Ohio Art Co., c. 1956. 13"h x 13¼" w x 7"d. **$125.00 – 175.00**.

The Little Orphan Annie electric range is in excellent condition. The label reads: "Louis Marx & Co., New York, N.Y. USA." The cord on most toy electric ranges wears as it protrudes from the connection. Marx devised a clamp that held the wire in place, preventing a frayed cord. Louis Marx & Co., c. 1930s. 8½"h x 9½"w x 5½"d. **$100.00 – 150.00**.

The Wolverine electric stove is rare. The off and on switches are pink, aqua, and red, complementing the light green stovetop; otherwise the structure is plain. 10¼"h x 11"w x 6"d. c. 1950. **$50.00 – 75.00**.

### *Non-Heating Stoves*

In the 1880s, the advertisement for cast-iron stoves stressed the fact that "fire can be built in this stove." By 1935, cast-iron stoves offered by Grey Iron offered this statement: "She can 'make believe' cook on them." Safety concerns were already in play. The late forties brought "electric" and "non-electric" stoves. The fifties, however, brought the great deluge of non-heating stoves. Wolverine, Ohio Art, Marx, Girard, and others gradually gained lead over the electric stoves. The post-war sheet steel stoves were colorful with litho designs.

This stove on legs has litho gas burners and early teardrop door pull. 9½"h x 10½"w x 5½"d. Wolverine Supply & Mfg. Co., Pittsburgh, Pennsylvania. **$40.00 – 65.00**.

This gas stove, cabinet style, was listed in Wolverine's 1942 catalog as "Modern Play Stove – Equipped with Utensils." It came with two spoons for hanging and two aluminum pans. 11⅞"h x 11"w x 6"d. **$60.00 – 75.00**.

Large Wolverine stove, No. 194/42. This is a handsome gas stove with litho burners and maroon base. The clock has metal hands; later ones were fiberboard. Very special is the pull-out drawer. Came with four aluminum pans and a "modern" tea kettle. 15¾"h x 14"w x 7¼"d. **$75.00 – 95.00**.

This blue and white stove is offered in Spiegel's 1950 catalog with this description: "heavy white enameled metal. Play stove has 4 plastic pans, working oven door." It is well anchored with a thick, heavy bottom. Wolverine, c. 1950. 15¼"h x 14"w x 7"d. **$50.00 – 75.00**.

Instead of litho burners usually found on Wolverine stoves, metal burners were added to this pink stove. A glowing red is visible underneath the burners. Wolverine, c. 1957. 12"h x 11"w x 6½"d. **$40.00 – 65.00**.

The packaging for this stove is unique. The stove back splash is lithoed with an oven thermometer, workable burner controls, automatic timer, and heat control indicator. Wolverine Toy Company, Pittsburgh, Pennsylvania. USA, 1960s. In box, unused, **$95.00**.

This red and white stove No. 188 has push buttons, litho salt and outlet, temperature controls, cooker well, and three burners. Wolverine, c. 1950. **$75.00 – 100.00**.

This stove is well built with an enclosed bottom, which makes it sturdy. All the buttons work, and the deep-well cooker is indicative of the modern post-World War stoves. Marx is one of the few companies that provided a removable deep-well cooker. The oven rack is plastic, suitable for cold cooking. Marx, 1950. 12½"h x 12"w x 6½"d. **$50.00 – 75.00**.

Snow White three-piece boxed set, refrigerator, sink, and stove, **$150.00 – 175.00**.

Snow White Refrigerator.

Snow White Sink.

Snow White Stove.

Ohio Art Play Stove with original plastic cookware. 5⅛"h x 8"w x 4½"d. 1956. **$55.00 – 85.00.**

### *Easy-Bake Oven*

By 1940, cast-iron toy stoves were slipping away; by the 1960s electric stoves were vanishing. On the horizon, however, loomed the "Easy-Bake Oven" that would take over. By 1968, this oven was shown on television and in most retail catalogs. It was a run-away bestseller. It cooked Betty Crocker mixes with energy from light bulbs. The box gives good information: "1970 Kenner Products Co. – Cincinnati, Ohio 45202, Made and printed in USA. Patent applied for." By 1974, it debuted in crimson red and today continues to be re-designed. Kenner Products Co., c. 1970s.

Easy-Bake Oven with pans. **$25.00 – 35.00**.

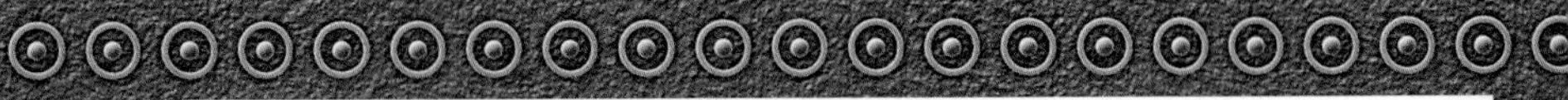

# KENNER'S
## Easy-Bake Oven

**A simple way for little girls to bake . . hands never touch the oven chamber**

Just slide cake tray into baking chamber here

When cake is done, slide thru cooling chamber . . hands never touch oven chamber

**$9.88** Easy-Bake unit with mixes and utensils

Young cooks 8 years old and up will love preparing and serving their own delicious desserts. They just choose a mix, add water and place in pan tray. Then slide tray into oven with handy pan pusher. When it's done (in about 14 minutes), push tray through cooling chamber and out. All pastries slide thru—oven door does not open—outside of oven stays cool.

Front panel has 2 knobs—one just for play and one is a real timing guide, just turn it to find the correct baking time for cookies, cakes or brownies. This 14½x6½x11-inch high polypropylene unit has baking chamber, cooling chamber, handy 2-shelf storage unit, 4 make-believe burners. Uses two 60-watt light bulbs (not incl.). UL listed for 110–120-volt, 60-cycle AC. Has three 4-in. round pans, 3 so-easy mixes. Fully assembled. Operating instructions incl.

- Bakes with just the heat from two 60-watt light bulbs
- Includes 3 pans and 3 "just-add-water"

**Easy-Bake Refill Set.** Includes 15 mixes: 8 cake mixes, 5 frosting mixes, 1 brownie and 1 gingerbread mix. Plus pans, bowl and spoon.

Shpg. wt. set 10 oz.

49 C 11061 ....... Set $3.79

Advertisement in Sears 1974 catalog.

# KITCHENWARE

### *Dolly's Kitchen Companions — Pots, Pans, Utensils, and Gadgets*

While many affluent families in the late nineteenth century provided their children with well-stocked Nuremburg kitchens, the average American play kitchen was not as composite. Generally, it consisted of a cupboard, table and chairs, a stove, and furnishings. Small pieces of adult furniture were often mixed with the toys. However, after World War I, vast selections of toy kitchen equipment such as ice boxes, refrigerators, cupboards, furnished grocery stores, and toy appliances of all descriptions appeared at affordable prices. Astonishing supplies of toy utensils in wood, tin, cast-iron, pewter, and aluminum were available.

### *Woodenware*

One of the oldest materials found in ancient playhouses is wood. It is much loved and respected. It is unadulterated. What you see is what it is; we feel safe with wood.

Many cultures had access to forests, which enabled prolific production of wooden objects. Germany, with her great forests, excelled in supplying the world with wooden toys and toy kitchenware from the early eighteenth century into the twentieth century.

Early eighteenth century doll kitchens reveal wooden equipage, such as baskets, barrels, churns, storage containers, tubs, chargers, bowls, salt boxes, butcher blocks, cutting boards, and many other wooden items. These were necessary, before the twentieth century, to maintain an adult kitchen and found their way into the play kitchen.

Kitchen Set. The pieces in this set were necessary for a well-furnished toy kitchen before the twentieth century. The salt box, a utensil carrier, a masher, a maul for tenderizing meats, a dough board, and a rolling pin for pastries make this set complete. Morton E. Converse & Son, c. 1900 – 1910. **$125.00**.

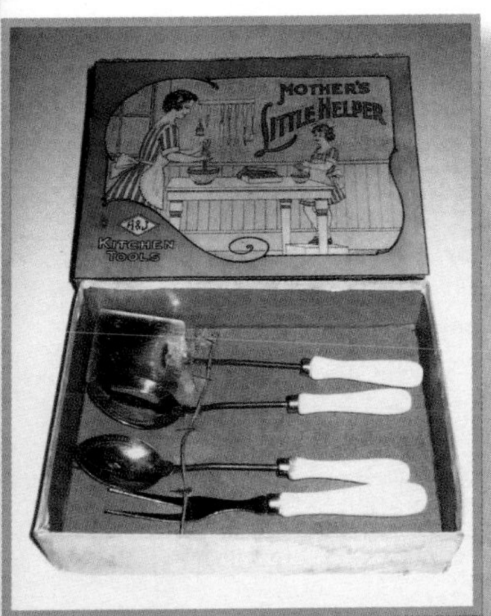


These kitchen sets with white handles are well crafted. Made by "A & J Mfg. Co." and packaged as "A & J Kitchen Tools" of Chicago, this company was aligned with Edward Katsinger Company, which produced abundant toy kitchenware. The set with green handles and little faces also is packaged as "A & J Kitchen Tools."

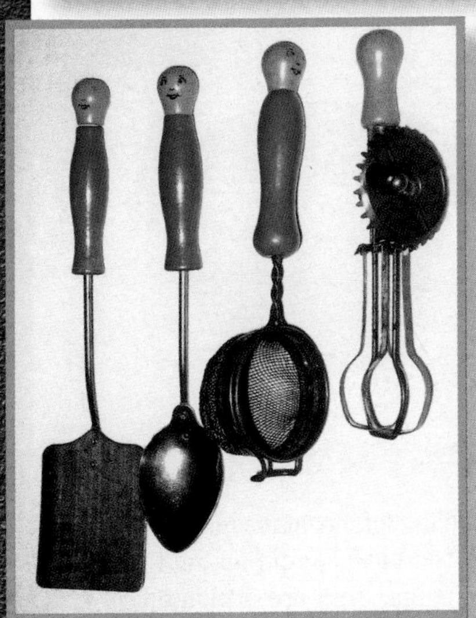

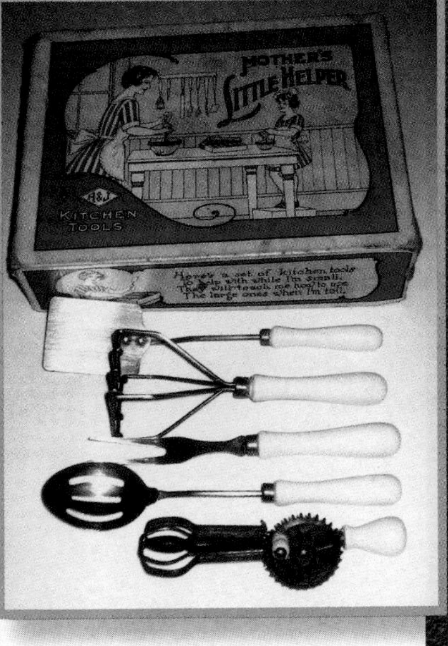


Small boxed set, **$45.00 – 65.00**.
Large boxed set, **$55.00 – 75.00**.
Green pieces, **$45.00**.

### *Cast-Iron Cookware*

America was foremost in the production of early toy iron cookware. In the nineteenth and twentieth centuries, most cast-iron toy cookstoves came supplied with utensils. In early years, J. & E. Stevens produced separate boxed assortments containing a skillet, spider, and kettle (pot). Kenton Toy Company also produced boxed sets.

The large, open, three-legged kettle on the left is embossed "Sugar Kettle." It measures 3¼" in diameter. The bailed kettle on the right is embossed "English Kettle," also on legs. Both are attributed to Kenton, c. 1910. Each, **$35.00**.

J. & E. Stevens utensils include a skillet on legs with one pouring lip, a kettle (pot), cake griddle, and lid lifter. These came with the Rival stove by J. & E. Stevens. **$75.00 – 100.00**.

Kenton utensils include an open skillet with no pouring lip, fry pan, and bailed kettle (pot). The small tea kettle is a quality piece. It has a slide lid with the knob cast in. Although the maker is unknown, it does have earmarks of early Kenton small tea kettles. **$100.00 – 125.00**.

The large kettle is by Kenton and labeled "Kenton Brand" on the bottom. The smaller kettle is by Kenton also. Large kettle, **$100.00 – 125.00**. Small kettle, **$100.00 – 125.00**.

### *Scales*

Scales have always been vital implements in adult kitchens. In the nineteenth century, much home canning and pickling were done. Many recipes called for measures in pounds. At this time, most food was still in bulk in grocery stores, and the housewife bought what she needed. It could be weighed again at home to see if the weight was correct. Into the early twentieth century, the dial scale with a pan on top and boxed-in mechanism became the favorite in the home.

Many companies, like Kenton, Arcade, Hubley, and others produced toy scales. By the 1930s, cast-iron scales were vanishing, but bake sets continued to include scales of varied materials into the 1960s.

Shown are two scales: Left: Kenton, 1920, **$75.00 – 100.00**. Right: A. C. Williams, c. 1914, **$65.00**.

***Mechanical Implements***

Among other kitchen implements needed before the rise of the modern kitchen were grinders and cast-iron waffle irons.

Left:
Daisy by Hubley, c. 1920. **$125.00**.

Center:
Little Tot by Arcade. L. H. Mace featured this grinder in 1907. It was still available in Arcade's 1929 catalog. **$125.00**.

Right:
The coffee mill was for grinding bulk coffee, usually done at a local grocery store. This Kenton bronze coffee mill with red trim is designed exactly like the commercial size with a hopper at the top and a pair of flywheels with a handle for turning. Kenton, c. 1910. **$75.00 – 100.00**.

## *Grinders*

Full-size food grinders were necessities in households before electricity. At hog killing time, rural folk depended on them for making sausage. Leftover meats were ground for meat pies. For heavy duty, the home grinder was made of nickeled iron or zinc.

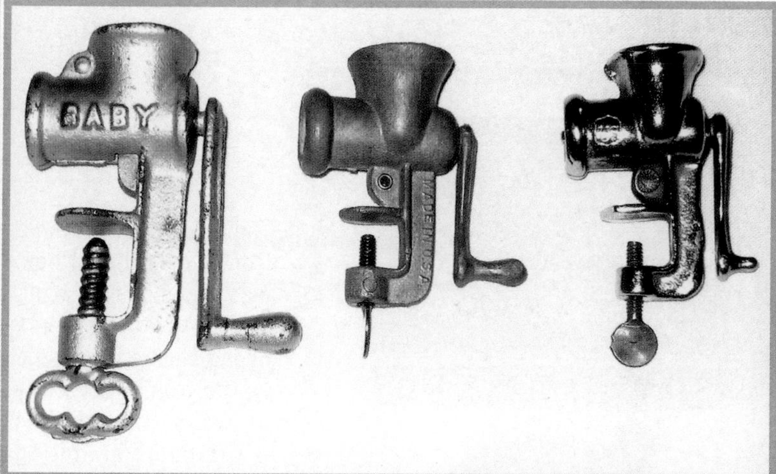


The Baby on the left is cast-iron by Hubley and silvered to imitate nickel. c. 1910. **$75.00**.

The Peerless in the center is pewter made by Peerless Mfg. Co. and imitates zinc. c. 1940. **$35.00**.

The heavy nickeled grinder on the right was made by a company proud to be American. "Made in USA" is embossed in bold letters on the standard with "US" embossed on the bowl. c. 1930. **$65.00**.

## *Waffle Irons*

Old nineteenth century companies, such as Griswold Mfg. Co. of Erie, Pennsylvania, Wagner Mfg. Co. of Sidney, Ohio, and Stover Mfg. & Engine Co. of Freeport, Illinois, had long furnished adult kitchens with cast-iron cookware. These companies produced junior size cookware in the 1920s. Junior cookware was too large for the ordinary toy stove and was used alongside Mother's on the kitchen range. Waffle irons fit into this category.

The Stover Junior Waffle Iron, with original box, was never played with. The sides of the box depict children using the waffle iron in a variety of ways. Included is a recipe flyer noting the advantages of the toy having been made "exactly like the famous Stover Waffle Iron." c. 1920. **$150.00 – 175.00**.

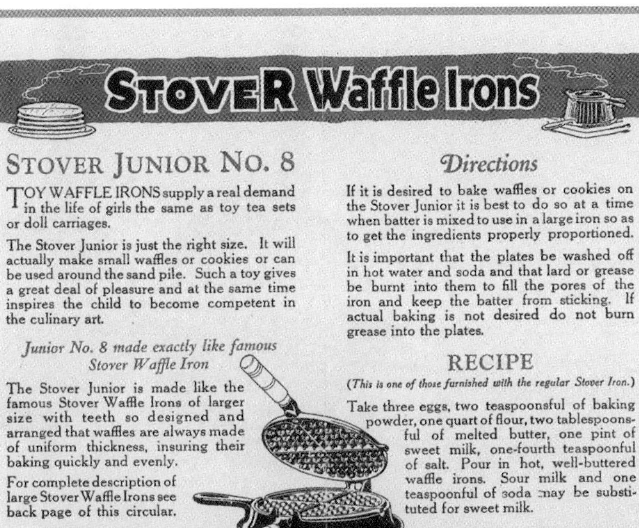

# STOVER Waffle Irons

## STOVER JUNIOR NO. 8

TOY WAFFLE IRONS supply a real demand in the life of girls the same as toy tea sets or doll carriages.

The Stover Junior is just the right size. It will actually make small waffles or cookies or can be used around the sand pile. Such a toy gives a great deal of pleasure and at the same time inspires the child to become competent in the culinary art.

*Junior No. 8 made exactly like famous Stover Waffle Iron*

The Stover Junior is made like the famous Stover Waffle Irons of larger size with teeth so designed and arranged that waffles are always made of uniform thickness, insuring their baking quickly and evenly.

For complete description of large Stover Waffle Irons see back page of this circular.

## *Directions*

If it is desired to bake waffles or cookies on the Stover Junior it is best to do so at a time when batter is mixed to use in a large iron so as to get the ingredients properly proportioned.

It is important that the plates be washed off in hot water and soda and that lard or grease be burnt into them to fill the pores of the iron and keep the batter from sticking. If actual baking is not desired do not burn grease into the plates.

## RECIPE

*(This is one of those furnished with the regular Stover Iron.)*

Take three eggs, two teaspoonsful of baking powder, one quart of flour, two tablespoonsful of melted butter, one pint of sweet milk, one-fourth teaspoonful of salt. Pour in hot, well-buttered waffle irons. Sour milk and one teaspoonful of soda may be substituted for sweet milk.

# STOVER

## Family Waffle Irons

Only those who use Stover Waffle Irons know the real pleasure of baking and eating high grade, evenly baked and delicious waffles.

The reason is this. The teeth on the Stover plates are so designed and arranged that they make the waffle of uniform thickness as shown by the cross section opposite.

The cross shaped teeth stand opposite the openings between the square shaped teeth and carry this formation to the outer edge of the pans. On other irons both plates have square shaped teeth, which stand opposite each other and form waffles that are very thick in some places and very thin in other places.

The Stover way results in the waffles baking quickly and evenly.

A big variety of waffles both hot or cold can be made on the Stover at a moderate cost. Each large size Stover Iron is sold with recipes that will give a big variety and selection.

| Wood Handles | Wire Handles | For Stove Hole |
|---|---|---|
| *Round* | | |
| 7 Low | 70 Low | 7 |
| 7 High | 70 High | 7 |
| 8 Low | 80 Low | 8 |
| 8 High | 80 High | 8 |
| 9 Low | 90 Low | 9 |
| 9 High | 90 High | 9 |
| *Square* | | |
| 28 Low | 280 Low | 8 |
| 28 High | 280 High | 8 |

Wire bails must be specified if wanted on round style.

For sale by dealers.

*Be sure you buy the Stover.*

Inserts that came with the Stover Junior Waffle Iron.

The Wagner bailed waffle iron is marked "Wagner 1892." The deep-grooved ring is for catching grease. Later models had no bail. c. 1900. **$75.00 – 100.00**.

Arcade featured two versions of the waffle iron. The rectangular one copies the family size popular in the 1870s. The one with round heads has green handles and base. The heads are "white plated." Issued in Arcade catalog (1929). Rectangular, c. 1920s. **$50.00 – 75.00**. Round, c. 1920s. **$125.00 – 150.00**.

***Tinware***

The use of tin is as old as time. Mixed with copper, it prevailed in the Bronze Age. It is known as "poor man's silver" because when new or protected from exposure, it is bright like silver.

Through the ages, tin was used in home and industry products to prevent rust. Even in the Middle Ages, acid food prepared in brass or copper containers often caused a dreaded poison called verdigris. It was learned that lining the vessel with tin prevented the problem. Many old copper and brass moulds in adult kitchens are lined with tin.

Tin was scarce during the Colonial period because it came from England saddled with high tariffs. By 1840, tin ore could be mined from newly established mines in Galena, Illinois. By the nineteenth century, tinware flooded kitchens with pudding pans, bread pans, pie pans, fry-pans, dairy pans, and other utensils. Play kitchens were well stocked with toy utensils as well.

Although tin is malleable and lightweight, it cannot be welded. It had to be joined with solder before stamping and rivets came into use in the late nineteenth century.

The sifter on the left with the red knob, c. 1930, is joined by rivets. **$30.00**.
In the center, the "Nesco" (National Enameling & Stamping Company) sifter, c. 1910, is soldered. The inside blades are thick. **$45.00**.
The wash boilers are examples of soldered tin, c. 1880 – 1890. **$65.00 each**.

Stamping became a shortcut, allowing many wares to be made without joining. It was known in Europe from the eighteenth century, in America c. 1880s. A patterned piece of tinplate or other metal was shaped and bent by a mechanical process to produce seamless adult or toy cookware. In one process, stamping could turn a circle into a bowl, wash pan, pie pan, or cake pan.

Examples of stamped toy utensils.
This seven-piece early tinware is heavy with rolled edges and presumed to be made by N.D. Cass Co. The pie pans have wooden pies and were included in a 1914 Cass cabinet. 7-piece set, **$75.00 – 95.00**.

**_Eggbeaters_**

The mechanical eggbeater was a welcomed invention where forks, wire whisks, wooden sticks, and paddles were used to beat and mix. By 1910, the eggbeater was a necessity in homes across America. The playhouse variety was soon to come.

The beater on the left is by A & J. The label reads: "Baby Bingo, No. 68, Pat. Apl'd for, USA." It is all metal and precedes the Betty Taplin model issued in 1923.
The one on the right is the next model issued. It has a wooden handle and is marked "Betty Taplin." **$20.00 – 30.00 each**.

***Jar Beaters***

Left:
Red knob and red handle, Betty Taplin. Glasbake bowl, 1920s – 1930s. **$100.00 – 125.00**.

Center:
Green knob and green handle, Betty Taplin. Bowl marked "Betty Taplin," c. 1920s – 1930s. **$100.00 – 125.00**.

Right:
This one is earlier, marked "A & J," and has an aqua and white knob with wire handle. Bowl is marked "Woolworth." **$100.00 – 125.00**.

### *Aluminum*

Aluminum is most often regarded as modern. However, it was discovered in France in the 1820s and, because it was expensive to extract from its ore, sold for $600 per pound. It became a novel metal and caused much excitement. Napoleon served his noble guests on aluminum tableware, aluminum being valued over silver and gold at that time.

Factories in France began pouring aluminum onto the market in the mid-nineteenth century. New refining techniques brought it to $2.25 per pound by 1890. This meant cheaper production costs for manufacturers because it was pliable and could be stamped easily. Not only did it fill adult kitchens in the late nineteenth and twentieth centuries, but aluminum also found a permanent place in playhouse kitchenware and tea sets.

In 1900, most toy kitchen sets were tin, but in 1911 Sears featured four different "Satin aluminum kitchen sets," noting that "Aluminum kitchen sets of late have become very popular." These toy sets were comprised of "pans, pails, cake dishes, covered and uncovered sauce pans, and frying pans."

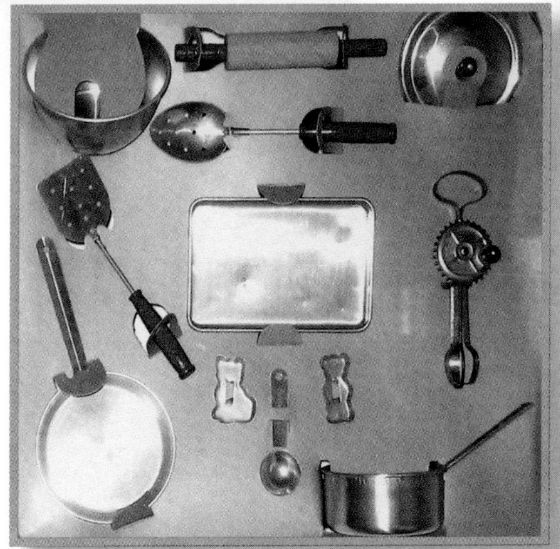

The Welker-Ware Aluminum Cooking Set produced by Welker Mfg. Co., Cromwell, Connecticut, features cooking and baking utensils. c. 1950. Complete boxed set, **$100.00**.

This cooking and baking set was available in the 1950s. Mirro Aluminum Co., Manitowoc, Wisconsin. Pieces shown, **$75.00 – 95.00**.

4.—19-PC. MINIATURE COOK SET: 6-cup biscuit pan, 4-in. mixing bowl, cake pan, frying pan, pie plate, jelly mold, 2 cake molds, 4 cookie cutters, cookie sheet, roaster and cover, measuring cup, scoop and 2 spoons.
35 J 6088. Polished Aluminum Set. (1 lb. 7 oz.)............... 19 Pcs. 1.19

In the 1930s and 1940s, cooking sets and baking sets were always offered separately. Cooking sets consisted mostly of pots and pans. Baking sets consisted of eggbeaters, bowls, cookie cutters, baking sheets, rolling pins, etc.

After World War II, aluminum was available again, and cooking and baking sets began to intermingle. In 1950, Spiegel offered a 19-piece "Miniature Cook Set" that included as many baking items as cooking items. Spiegel catalog reprint.

This kitchen set was advertised in Butler Brothers, 1930. Many pieces were used with the Kokomo electric ranges. This set includes tube cake pan, 4¼" diameter, 4" double roaster, and other pieces "in proportion." In 1931, the oval roaster replaced the double roaster and remains the same pattern today. This set is missing a double boiler. Probably Aluminum Specialty Co., Manitowoc, Wisconsin, c. 1930s. **$75.00 – 100.00**.

The Miniature Cast Aluminum Cooking Utensils set is a treasured find. The owner gave valuable information: "I was born in 1934 and received the set in 1940." Made by F. & S. Products Co. of Dayton, Ohio. The larger vessels measure 3" in diameter, smaller ones 2½" in diameter. **$125.00 – 150.00**.

The Copper Clad Revere Ware Stainless Steel sets have been made in eight-piece and twelve-piece sets. All the pieces are marked and are copies of the adult size. Extremely well made, they are heavy pieces with a bake-o-lite type handle with rings for hanging. Revere Copper & Brass, Inc., Rome Mfg. Div., Rome, New York, c. 1950. 12-piece set, **$125.00 – 175.00**.

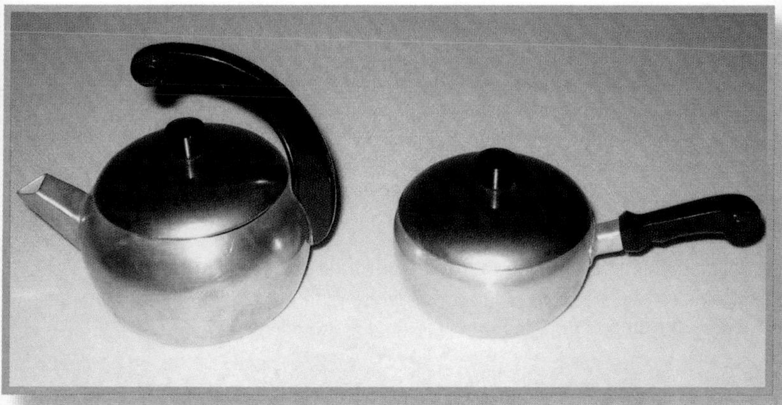

The Junior Hallite sets are known to have been made in six-piece and nine-piece sets. The six-piece set consists of skillet, saucepan with cover, ladle, spatula, and cooking fork. The pieces clearly note: "WEAREVER, Made only by Wolverine, Made in U.S.A., Pittsburgh, Pa., HALLITE JUNIOR." c. 1950. Saucepan with lid, **$30.00**. Skillet, **$20.00**.

### *Graniteware*

When graniteware, also called enamelware and agateware, was demonstrated at the Philadelphia Centennial Exposition in 1876, it was pushed and promoted by the manufacturers hoping it would take over all other housewares. Comparing it to the ruler of cookware, cast-iron, it was to bring relief to heavy cast-iron lifting, scrubbing, and cleaning. It would also abolish the chore of cleaning and polishing copper and brass. It was to be the great benefactor of leisure time. In the 1940s, however, it began to lose favor with the housewife. Chips and dents weakened the metal, and chips inside the vessel would splinter in stirring. It was prized if perfect.

By the 1870s, three major areas, Sheboygan, Wisconsin; Woodhaven, New York; and St. Louis, Missouri, became centers of production. From these factories came graniteware bearing paper labels. Very few companies burned the label into the product. It is difficult to distinguish the maker after the label is removed. White with black, blue, or red trim, as well as mottled gray, is often classified as American.

The pie plate and bailed kettle are copies of American adult pieces; they are attributed to Lisk Mfg. Co., c. 1920s. Pie plate, **$35.00**. Kettle, **$45.00**.

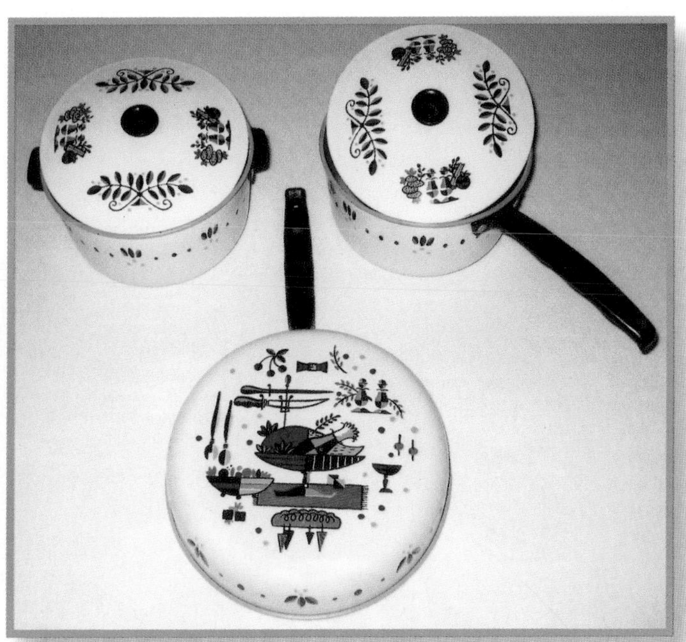

The late 1950s and 1960s brought on litho cooking sets mainly by Wolverine. These sets were for cold cooking. This set was shown in Spiegel's 1964 catalog as "Fiesta-Ware" and scaled for "Rite Hite Appliances." Saucepan with lid, 4¾" diameter. Dutch oven with lid, 4¾" diameter. Skillet, 6" diameter. Five pieces, **$50.00 – 85.00**.

The 1970s and 1980s brought more and more plastic to the marketplace. Cast-iron, electric, and other heating stoves were vanishing by the 1960s. Plastic cookware was suitable for non-heating stoves, and found a permanent place in the play kitchen.

This Corning Ware cooking set gives valuable information: "Aluminum Specialty Company, Manitowoc, Wis." (Chilton Toys). "Cornflower Set with toy plastic replicas of CORNINGWARE Products." Special license was granted to Aluminum Specialty Co. by "CORNING GLASS WORKS – DO NOT PUT NEAR HEAT." c. 1958. **$95.00**.

# Household Furnishings with Name-Brand Products

In the early 1900s, American toymakers broke new ground in advertising when they began to use toy grocery stores, toy kitchen cabinets, and other toy furniture as conveyors to advertise name-brand products. This new form of advertising proved profitable for both toy and food enterprises. Familiar packages, such as Wheatena, Argo Starch, Bon Ami, S.O.S. soap pads, and Life Buoy soap filled toy grocery stores and toy furniture.

Building on this new idea was the N.D. Cass Company. Scant information is given in toy books on this late nineteenth century woodworking firm of Athol, Massachusetts. I was fortunate to connect with Richard Chaisson, Athol Town Historian and former reporter for the *Athol Daily News*, who had worked with Cass while in school the summer of 1951: "I was hired as a stock boy with added duties as a paint dipper (taking the finished, but unpainted, toys down from the overhead conveyor belt and drowning every single one of them in a bathtub-sized vat of dope [chemical] paint), assembler (using a hammer and screwdriver to fasten toy parts together), and general errands runner."

The company began operation in 1896, making travel cases and fiberboard boxes. By the early 1900s, Cass became aware of "potential in the toy market." The company began producing wooden trains, trucks, ironing boards, and kitchen toys, especially kitchen cabinets. The cabinets were copies of the real cabinets found in American kitchens in the early twentieth century.

In 1952, a factory opened in Brent, Alabama, and remained the only one in operation after the plant in Athol closed. The Brent plant specialized in juvenile furniture, rather than smaller Cass toys. After a tornado brought it down in 1973, it was rebuilt, and in 1997, employed almost 300 people. Companies like Toys-R-Us, Wal-Mart, J.C. Penney, Sears, and others patronized N.D. Cass.

I was able to get in touch with employees of the Brent plant to learn that the company closed in 2001. This was a great American company that hardly has a footnote in collectors' books, but many of its toys are in collections today.

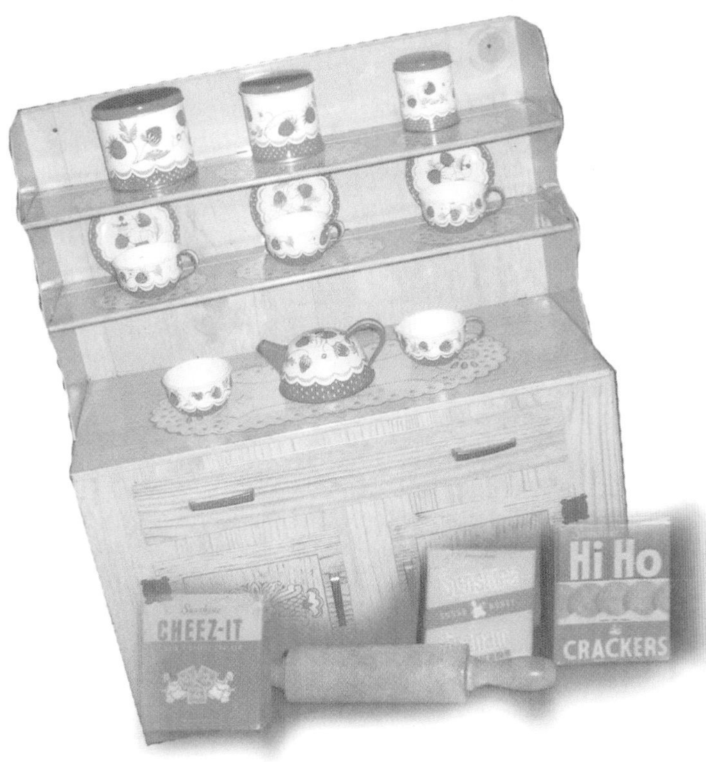

### *Cass Kitchen Cabinets*

In 1914, Butler Brothers advertised four different Cass cabinets. They ranged from 14" – 21" in height. Each of the four cabinets came with a "large supply of facsimile pkgs., groceries, some filled." Each also came with a "bake board, rolling pin and potato masher." As the cabinets increased in size, more items were added.

This cabinet (17"l x 5"w x 21"h) has the flour bin so well-identified in American adult kitchens in the 1920s – 1940s. N.D. Cass Company, 1914. **$225.00 – 350.00**.

Butler Brothers' 1914 catalog described this Cass cabinet: "13½"l x 6"w x 16"h, china spice jar, rolling pin, bake board, potato masher, flour bin with scoop." It came with name-brand packages and is special because of the flour bin on such a small cabinet. The two pie pans filled with wooden pies are original with some Cass cabinets. **$150.00 – 200.00**.

This smaller Cass cabinet is extremely well-crafted. It is unique in that the bake board fits between two grooves on top of the work-space, whereas in other Cass cabinets, the bake board usually fits underneath the workspace. N.D. Cass Company, 1912. 13¼"l x 5"w x 15½"h. **$100.00 – 150.00**.

# Household Furnishings with Name-Brand Products

This cream and green cabinet depicts popular colors for the 1930s. Two decals show a little girl in an apron holding a large tea kettle. Name-brand packages came with the cabinet also. American, maker unknown, c. 1930. 12"l x 4¼"w x 15½"h. **$35.00 – 55.00**.

### *Wolverine Cabinets and Cupboards*

Emphasized in this text is the enormous toy housekeeping line produced by Wolverine Supply & Mfg. Company of Pittsburgh, Pennsylvania. These toys represent a variety of stoves, sinks, refrigerators, washing machines, cleaning sets, tea sets, salad sets, and more.

The company was established in 1903 by Benjamin F. Bain as tool and die operation. Wolverine agreed to tool a sand toy for a company that failed, and Wolverine was left with tooling for sand toys. The company then developed an impressive line of "Sandy Andy" toys and a large line of housekeeping toys.

In 1968, Wolverine became a subsidiary of Spang Industries and the name was changed to Wolverine Toy Company. The company was moved to a new location in Booneville, Arkansas, in December 1970. In 1984, the product line changed somewhat, and the company became known as Today's Kids. In 1999, the name changed to Today's Plastics, with Wolverine moving one step further away from its previous identity. In June 2003, the announcement was made: "Today's Plastics to close by July 31." The last remnant of Wolverine was gone.

Wolverine offered several cabinets with food packages from the late 1930s to the late 1960s. In the 1942 catalog, the company listed "Kitchen Cabinets Filled with Famous Food Packages." The large deluxe model contained a bread board, rolling pin, eggbeater, bowl, muffin pan, and ten packages. The packages included Sunshine Krispy Crackers, Lava Soap, Worcester Salt, S.O.S., Rit Dye, Brillo Soap Pads, K.O., Junket, etc. In 1950, Spiegel ran the same cabinet with a reduced number of packages and cooking items. Wolverine, 1940s, 17"l x 10½"w x 20"h. **$250.00 – 325.00**.

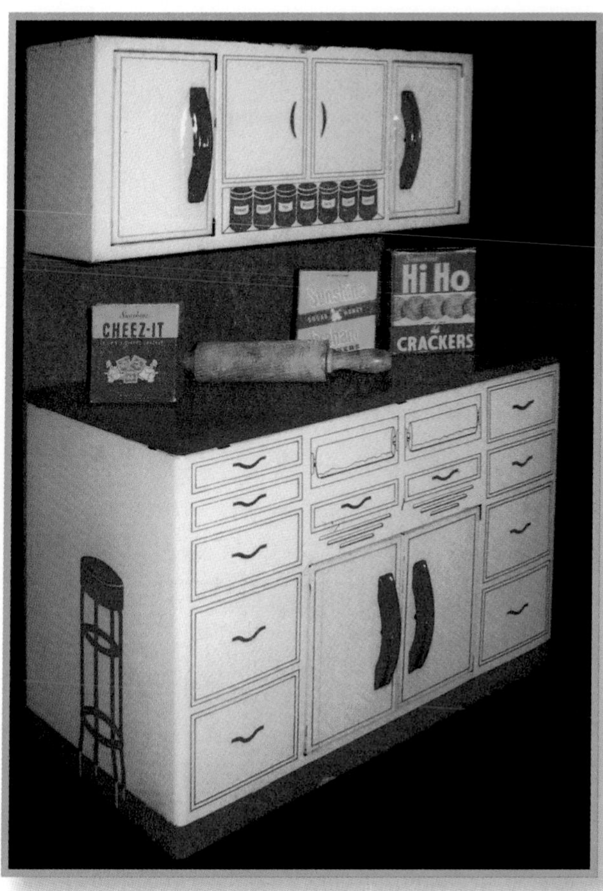


This cabinet came with all products shown. The kitchen stool lithoed on each side is a special feature. Wolverine, c. 1948, 11"l x 6½"w x 15¾"h. **$65.00 – 95.00**.

During the late 1950s and 1960s, everything made for a little girl's kitchen could be found in pink. Sun Maid Raisins, Jack Frost Sugar, and rolling pin are original with cabinet. Wolverine, c. 1960s. 11"l x 6½"w x 15¾"h. **$55.00 – 75.00**.

The cinnamon-colored cabinet was popular when avocado and tangerine colors were advertised. It is sturdily built with an enclosed bottom. Wolverine, c. 1960s. 11"l x 6½"w x 15¾"h. **$35.00 – 55.00**.

## Old English Hutch Cabinet

(M) So handsome in little girl's "kitchen" with pretty tea set and canisters on its 3 shelves. Steel cabinet lithographed in knotty pine design. Top drawer opens with 2 brass pulls. Two bottom doors swing open; have brass hinges, pulls.

Accessories are steel, enameled white with red and green strawberry design. Includes 3 varied size canisters, 3 cups, 3 saucers, sugar, creamer, and teapot.

48 T 4656 M—20½x17x6¾ in. Wt. 8 lbs. 4.98

By the mid-fifties, Wolverine's cabinets had moved up in size. In 1957, this "Old English Cupboard" was offered with the popular strawberry three-piece canister set, three cups, three saucers, sugar, creamer, and teapot. Wolverine, 17"l x 7"w x 20½"h . Cupboard, **$40.00 – 65.00**. Cupboard with canister set and tea set, **$175.00 – 225.00**.

Probably the last Wolverine cupboard in this style was the 1968 model issued — "Colorful and charming Tyrolean scenes decorate this all steel cabinet." Wolverine, c. 1966. 17"l x 7"w x 20½"h. **$45.00 – 65.00**.

Thalhimers' 1953 catalog described this cabinet as, "All the warmth, color and charm of old Pennsylvania Dutch design. Contains 40 pieces, plastic tea service, everything needed for baking and having a party." A different feature from the Wolverine models is the heavy plastic segmented drawer. Accessories are not original with the cupboard, but are made by Ideal. The label on the cabinet reads: "Made in USA. Ideal Toy Corp., Hollis 7, N.Y." 1953. 17"l x 6¾"w x 20½"h. **$45.00 – 70.00**.

**TC-16H—CHINA CABINET** by Ideal. All the warmth, color and charm of old Pennsylvania Dutch design. Contains 40 pieces, plastic tea service; everything needed for baking and having a party....................................5.98

### *Wolverine Grocery Stores*

A modern grocery store emerged in the 1920s. Wolverine came out with two beautiful lithoed stores, The Corner Grocer and General Grocery. The people, store design, and packages give valuable history of the times.

The Corner Grocer measures 31" wide x 14½" high and the counter is 15⅞" long. There are no people featured in this model. The products shown are original with the store. Wolverine, 1930s – 1940s. **$250.00 – 300.00**.

The General Grocery has litho on two wings and two shelves in the center. This model is more difficult to find. It is smaller than the Corner Grocer, measuring 20¼" wide, 12" high, and the counter is 10¼" long. The awning is a special feature. Wolverine, 1930s – 1940s. Products shown are original with store. **$175.00 – 250.00**.

A progression of Wolverine refrigerators is shown. The earliest one, c. 1938, has the blue and white "Polar" logo, plain tin corrugated shelves, and a teardrop door lock. It has a metal ice tray and six ice cubes (six silvered wooden blocks). All products shown are original with this model. Wolverine, c. 1938. 8"l x 5⅜"w x 13½"h. **$75.00 – 100.00**.

This is the same refrigerator as on the previous page but with a red and white logo and a different lock on the door, a slide lock. The shelves, rather than being corrugated tin, are white litho. Wolverine, c. 1940s. 8"l x 5⅜"w x 13½"h. **$35.00 – 55.00**.

The modern model came out in the late forties and was shown in Spiegel (1950). There are two doors, one for opening the refrigerator, one for opening the freezer compartment; the one-door refrigerator was gone. The litho door had been reduced from 8" to 7¼". Products had changed to include play food and canned fruit and juice with Wolverine labels. 8"l x 5⅜"w x 13½"h. **$35.00 – 55.00** without products. **$55.00 – 75.00** with products.

The green refrigerator has one stationary shelf and one revolving shelf. It is heavy and larger than other refrigerators shown in this text. 9¾"l x 6½"w x 16¾"h. Wolverine, c. 1960s. **$55.00 – 95.00**.

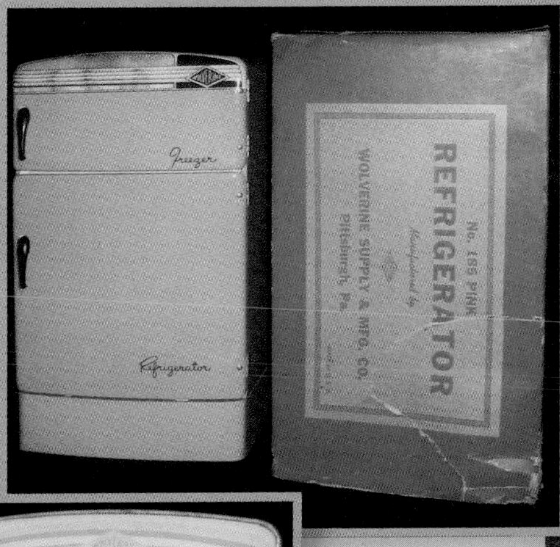

No. 185 pink refrigerator with box is labeled: "Wolverine Supply & Mfg. Co., Pittsburgh, Pa. Made in USA." It has the overall measurements of the one-door models. The litho door changed designs with this model. The door indicates changes in consumer habits of Americans. Previous doors show very few bottled products; they are abundant in this model. 8"l x 5⅜"w x 13½"h, c. 1957. **$75.00 – 100.00**.

Wolverine produced packages of foodstuffs using its own label; each bears the company logo. These products include:

- White Leghorn Eggs
- Extra Lean Bacon
- Fresh Creamery Butter
- Can of Ripe Red Cherries
- Can of Hawaiian Pineapple Juice
- Can of Concentrated Orange Juice

Other products shown do not have Wolverine labels but came with Wolverine refrigerator. **$15.00 – 25.00 each**.

## *Sinks*

In the late twenties, Sears offered adult kitchen sinks with single or double drainboards and two cast-iron legs, but no cabinet style. By the late thirties, the new cabinet style was becoming a permanent fixture in average American kitchens.

Although Wolverine stoves, cupboards, and refrigerators changed styles regularly, the sink stayed the same. The main attraction was the working faucet and an "adjustable stopper" in the basin. In 1942, Wolverine declared, "This substantial-size new sink looks as if it were taken right out of the pages of the latest periodicals on smart home decorations." By the 1960s, the single Wolverine sink was moving out of production.

This sink on legs is a late 1930s model. Later sinks were always cabinet style. Special features are the litho glasses on either side and the well-constructed metal soap dish. Water from a reservoir in back pours from the two faucets. The striking colors and special features make this a very desirable toy. Wolverine, c. 1938. 9½"h x 10½"w x 5½"d. **$55.00 – 85.00**.

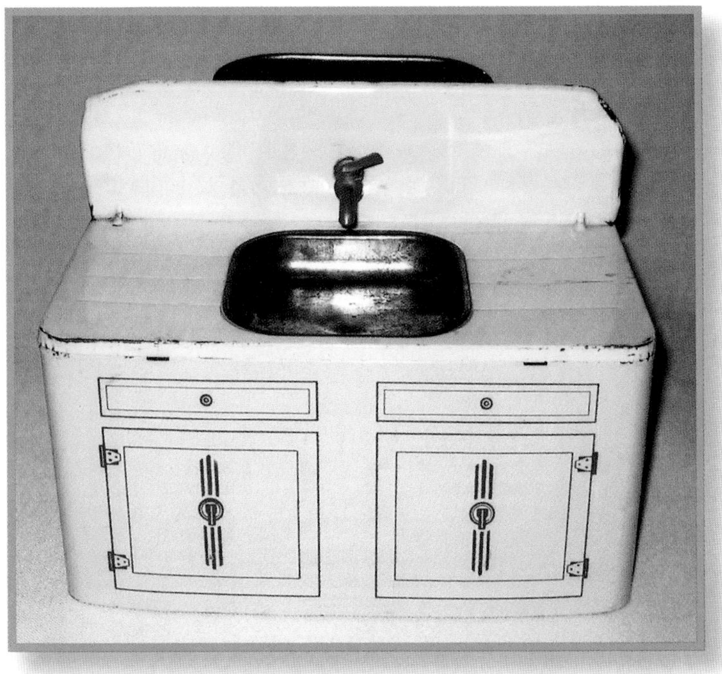

This small sink, 5½" x 7½", c. 1940, is in excellent condition and, because of its size, is more expensive than the larger model. In 1942, Wolverine advertised the: "Modern Running-Water Cabinet Sink." **$65.00 – 75.00**.

The pink sink, No. 197, has a moveable plug. The pink color adds interest, and the box is a valuable document, c. 1950s. With box, **$75.00 – 100.00**.

***Amsco – American Metal Specialties Corp.***

This company of Hatboro, Pennsylvania, is a name well-trusted in the toy world. The design and construction of Amsco toys can be relied upon for quality and fine details. Excepting the first blue Doll-E-Nurser, Amsco's Doll-E sets contained name-brand product packages. The company produced beautiful enamelware pieces in early sets, and paper labels are often found on these pieces. The 1950s were very successful years for the company.

In the sixties, Amsco was ever challenged by Mattel's Barbie® and her own accessories. Montgomery Ward and Sears' constant innovations in using their own brands for play housekeeping and baby doll care cut into demand for Amsco toys. In 1970, the company was acquired by Milton Bradley. Amsco toys seem destined to increase in value and appreciation.

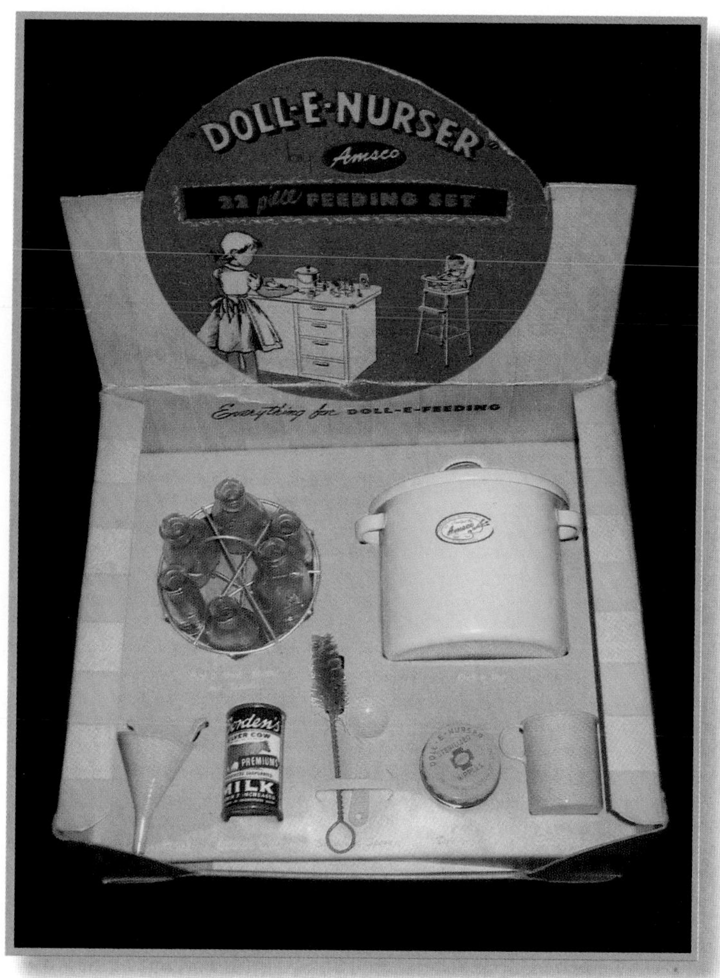


Doll-E-Nurser 22-piece feeding set is an early set with paint palette logo. The Borden's evaporated milk can is special and seldom seen. Amsco, c. 1948. Mint in box, **$125.00 – 150.00**.

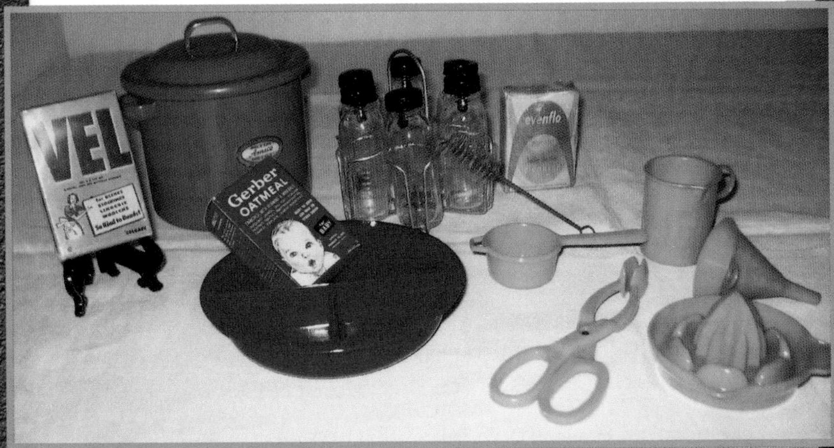


The Doll-E-Feeder consists of green enamel sterilizer, measuring cup, six Evenflo bottles with rubber nipples and bake-o-lite style caps, red feeding plate, yellow funnel, yellow forceps, yellow juicer, Vel, and Gerber oatmeal. Amsco, 1953. Pieces shown, **$100.00 – 125.00**.

The Doll-E-Feedette has 12 pieces: dish, four napkins, spoon, bottle with nipple, strainer, milk bottle with stopper, Gerber's oatmeal, Evenflo cleanser, and bib. Amsco, 1955. Boxed set, **$125.00**.

The Doll-E-Do-Dish set contains a brush, dish mop, green enamel dishpan, rack, strainer, polishing cloth, DuPont sponge, Ajax, Vel, and Brillo soap pads. Polishing cloth not shown. Amsco, 1953. **$75.00 – 100.00**.

The twenty-seven-piece Kidd-E-Kitchen is complete with dishpan, rack, sink strainer, plastic apron, Plasco tea set, and flatware, Rubbermaid drain mat, Ajax, Vel, Brillo, DuPont sponge, and Morgan-Jones dish towel – all name-brand products. Amsco, 1953. Boxed set, **$175.00**.

Doll-E-Housekeeper contains 14 pieces: pail, broom, sweeper, cleaning brush, apron, dustmop, dustpan, scrub brush, Gold Seal Congoleum Rug, Ajax, Vel, Brillo, DuPont sponge, and box for cabinet. Amsco, 1953. Boxed set, **$175.00 – 225.00**.

Another view of the Doll-E-Housekeeper.

# BAKING DAY

One of the earliest methods of baking in the Colonies was using the bake-kettle or Dutch oven, laid in the fireplace. Afterwards, ovens were built inside the fireplace or in an outside bake shed. There was very little baking a child could do, and child's play was very limited. By the 1870s, however, cast-iron toy stoves designed to contain real fire opened the way for slight baking in the toy oven. Some children were allowed to add small baking pans in Mother's oven.

Mrs. Louise Hoy Wells recalls playing with dough in the 1900s: "I didn't have a play stove. But on baking days, Mother would give me pinches of dough that I could shape. I did have a little bread pan and pie pan and would fill them with scrap dough and make and imprint with a fork on top of the dough. After Mother's baking was removed from the oven, and the oven had cooled a little, my dough was put inside to bake. They would burn if not carefully attended."

Prior to 1900, pastry sets came with only a bread board and rolling pin. Soon, a masher was added, and this comprised the pastry set until the early 1900s. By 1910, a small wooden bowl was added and the rolling pin had "stained red handles." More pieces continued to be added over time.

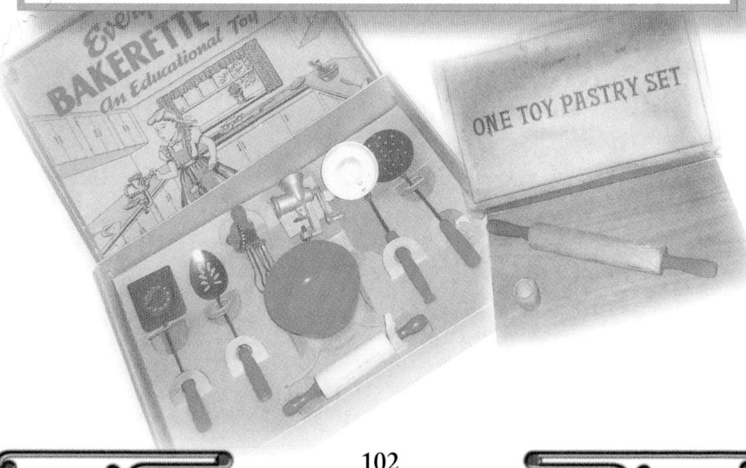

Early pastry set with bread board, rolling pin, and small wooden mixing bowl. Morton E. Converse & Son, Winchendon, Massachusetts, c. 1900 – 1910. **$55.00 – 75.00**.

Little Helper Pastry Set. The box states, "Manufactured By Newton & Thompson Inc., Brandon, VT. USA." Newton & Thompson made many wooden kitchen sets, ironing boards, and other small wooden toys. The inside of the top lid gives a list of "Cooking Suggestions" and a "Basic Cake Recipe." The glass bowl is Hazel-Atlas. The wooden contents have stained handles and designs, c. 1930s. **$65.00 – 95.00**.

Packaged as Wolverine Cake Box Set No. 260. Blue Delph design, 1948. Boxed set, **$200.00 – 275.00**.

This bake set is based on Wolverine's No. 256 set, which has a metal rectangular tray for a bread board, and a large plate, 4⅞" in diameter, labeled "cake plate." The dinner plate is 4" in diameter. Missing are the four mixing spoons. c. 1957. Pieces shown, **$150.00 – 175.00**.

This Tea and Baking Set has a metal pastry board rather than a wooden board. Wolverine, Strawberry design, c. 1950s. Based on Wolverine's No. 259 set. Pieces shown, **$175.00 – 200.00**.

A colorful set consisting of: pastry board; cookie sheet; rolling pin; three bowls (blue, yellow, and red); four-piece canister set; and two pie pans. Missing mixing spoon and shell mold. Ohio Art Co., 1956. Pieces shown, **$175.00 – 250.00**.

This bright yellow set with gold stars and red tops was called a Tea and Bake Set with canisters and tea set. Wolverine, c. 1960s. (A bread box was also available). Pieces shown, **$100.00 – 150.00**.

Cinderella Pastry Set is a complete set containing a scale with weights, not often seen in pastry sets. The box denotes: "Copyright, MXML, Peerless Playthings Company, Inc., New York, Made in U.S.A., Printed in U.S.A," 1950. Boxed set, **$75.00 – 100.00**.

This Hansel and Gretel Cookie Cutter Set features Hansel, Gretel, tree from the forest, gingerbread house, and witch, all in brilliant red plastic. The inside box cover tells the story of the Grimm's fairy tale. Recipes are included. Educational Products Co., 516 Fifth Ave., N.Y. 18 U.S.A., 1947. Boxed set, **$45.00 – 55.00**.

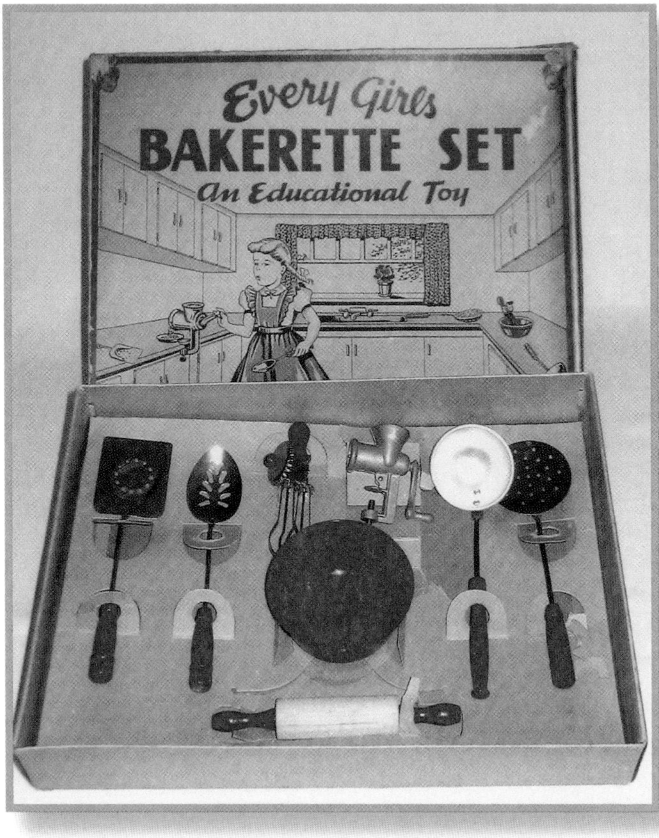

Bakerette Set, marked "Baker Mfg. Co., Columbia, PA. No. 100, Made in U.S.A.," c. 1950. Boxed set, **$95.00**.

Junior Chef Cake Mix Set. This set was produced by Argo Industries Corp., New York, New York, U.S.A., 1956. Boxed set, **$75.00 – 100.00**.

Junior Cookie Maker by Kay Stanley, Model Craft, Inc., 1017 W. Washington Blvd., Chicago 7, IL, c. 1950. Packaged set, **$35.00 – 55.00**.

The Dessert Set with Real Food contains Jell-O desserts and Pillsbury Pie Crust Mix. Kay Stanley, 1955. Boxed set, **$100.00 – 150.00**.

Cake Mix Set by Kay Stanley, Model Craft, Inc., c. 1955. Complete boxed set, **$75.00 – 100.00**.

Betty's Pastry Set. Transogram Company, Inc., "A Gold Medal Toy." Special items, two Hazel-Atlas bowls and a Hazel-Atlas "Lemon" flavoring bottle. Complete boxed set, **$75.00 – 125.00**.

Betty Jane 9-piece baking set, oval baking dish, bread pan, covered casserole, pie plate, and four custard cups. Glasbake, 1940s. Complete boxed set, **$125.00 – 175.00**.

Sunny Suzy Glass Baking Set by Wolverine, No. 260, c. 1940s. All pieces are marked "Fire-King Oven Glass." Contains four custard cups and open and covered casseroles. By Anchor Hocking for Wolverine. These pieces can be assembled from adult Anchor Hocking pieces, so the box is a must in defining this set as a toy set. 7-piece boxed set, **$125.00 – 150.00**.

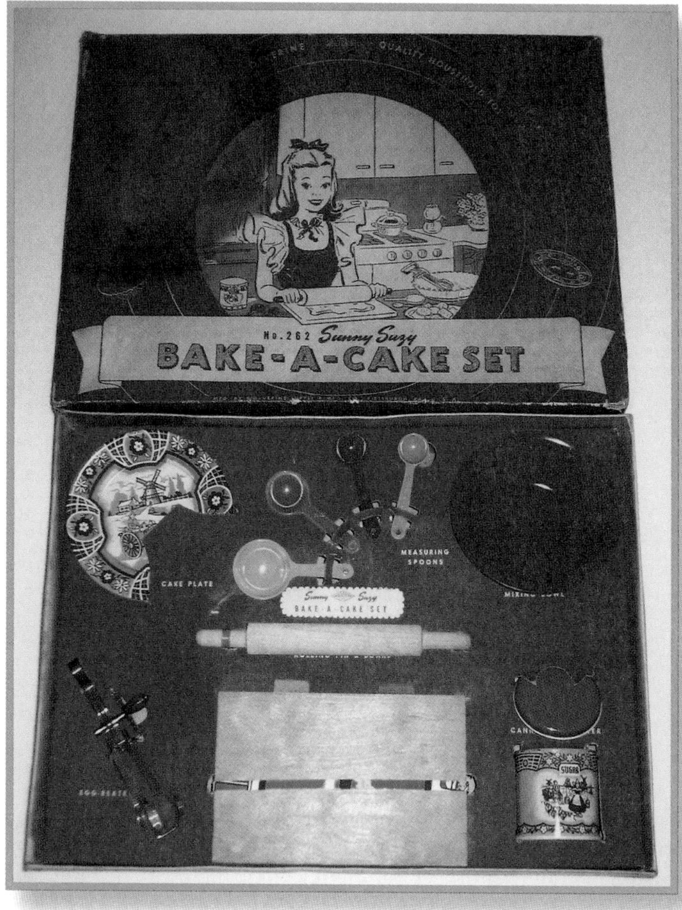


The Sunny Suzy Bake-A-Cake Set by Wolverine contains the $4\frac{7}{8}$" plate labeled "Cake Plate," which is $\frac{7}{8}$" larger than the 4" dinner plate. Only the sugar canister came with this set. **$75.00 – 125.00**.

Little Mother's Pastry Set is by J. Pressman & Co., New York, New York. It contains two cake pans, bread board, rolling pin, potato masher, and a tiny mixing bowl. c. 1935. **$35.00 – 55.00**.

This colorful Pastry Set, marked "Made in USA No. 5902," is also by J. Pressman. The two cake forms are lithoed a deep maroon inside and gold outside. The entire contents are near mint. The pastry board is labeled "Small Fry" and a special recipe book, *Recipes for the Small Fry*, was produced by Welch's Grape Juice Co., c. 1940s. **$100.00 – 125.00**.

### BISCUIT TARTS

Make baking powder biscuits with your favorite recipe or prepared biscuit mix. Roll or pat biscuits thinner than usual — about $\frac{1}{8}$ inch thick. Cut out with biscuit cutter. On half of each biscuit place a teaspoon of your favorite Welch Jelly or Preserve, fold the other half of biscuit over until the edge meets the lower half. Crimp edges with a fork. Bake as usual. Serve hot.

### BLACKBERRY JAM CAKE

3 eggs, 1 cup sugar, $\frac{3}{4}$ cup oleo, $2\frac{1}{4}$ cups flour, 1 cup Welch's Blackberry Jam, 1 teaspoon nutmeg, 1 cup raisins, $\frac{1}{2}$ cup pecans, 1 teaspoon baking powder, 3 tablespoons buttermilk and $\frac{1}{2}$ teaspoon soda

Mix all together and bake in greased pan in moderate oven.

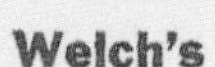

In the late 1950s, bake sets of enormous content were advertised. Sears (1962) hit the top with "Our big 120-piece Junior Chef Food Mix Set." By the 1970s, the market was calming down, and Sears only offered a 65-piece Mix and Utensil Set.

Sears advertisement, 1962.

# Cleaning Day

The Indians taught early settlers to make sturdy brooms from birch saplings splintered at the ends and applied to sapling branches. If wild grasses were available, a broom could be made by binding the grass at one end and using the flexible ends for sweeping. Corn shucks tied to a stick served also. The broom has been a necessary utility through the ages.

With the Victorian Age came preoccupation with hygiene and getting rid of dust that could carry germs. Every household was well-supplied with brushes, brooms, dustpans, and cleaning products.

By the early 1900s, the broom was being moved aside for a new invention, the carpet sweeper. Invented by Anna and Melville Bissell in 1876, by 1890 it was known the world over. Queen Victoria furnished Buckingham Palace with Bissell carpet sweepers.

**_Toy Carpet Sweepers_**

Prior to 1900, few toy carpet sweepers were available. In 1905, John Wannamaker Dept. Store advertised the toy Bissell in three different sizes. In 1914, Butler Brothers listed "Child's Bissell" and "Little Queen."

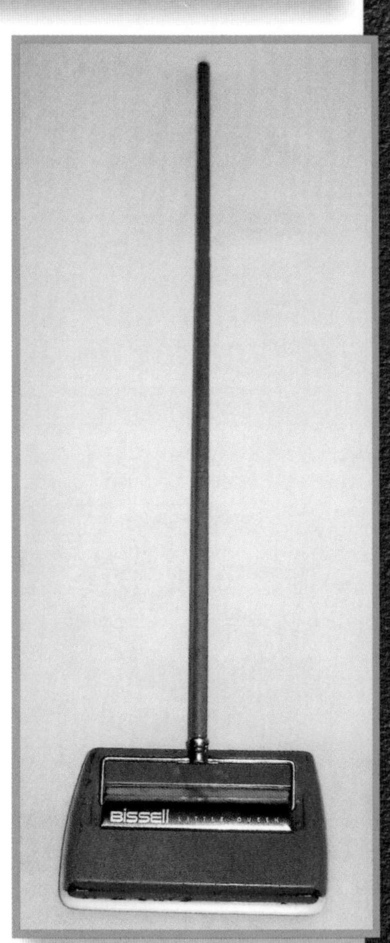


Of heavy metal construction, this Bissell labeled "Little Queen" is given a good description in a 1957 catalog: "All steel case, genuine bristle brush, rubber tired wheels, vinyl bumper, three-piece sectional handle and large dust pan that actually empties." Bissells were sold individually or with other accessories in a set. This sweeper sold as a single item, 1957. **$45.00 – 65.00**.

**BISSELL LITTLE QUEEN CARPET SWEEPER**

Made to look and work, just like Mother's . . . and gee, it really sweeps. All steel case, genuine bristle brush, rubber-tired wheels, vinyl bumper, three-piece sectional handle, and large dust pan that actually empties. Ages 5 to 10.

Little Queen Carpet Sweeper..................$2.98

Reprint page from Rucker-Rosenstock catalog, 1957.

An unusual feature with this sweeper is a dustpan that fits in a slot on the front of the sweeper. Gotham Pressed Steel Corp., New York, c. 1950. **$45.00 – 65.00**.

This attractive litho sweeper depicts a demonstration of how the dustpan is used with the sweeper. "Norstar, Little Handi-Aid." Norstar, Bronx, New York, 1950. **$55.00 – 85.00**.

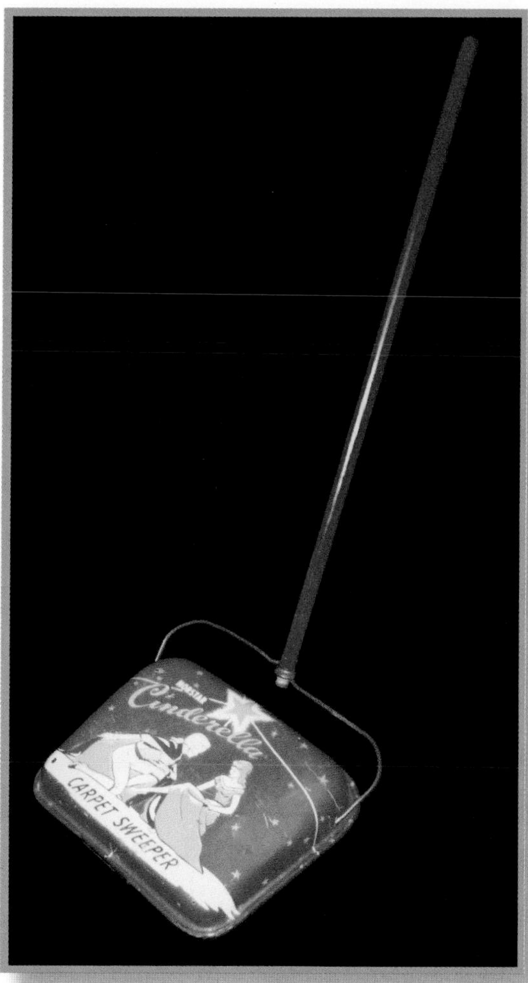


The Cinderella Carpet Sweeper came in a cleaning set with broom, dustpan, and floor mop, 1951. By 1953, the broom and mop changed styles, but the carpet sweeper stayed the same. Norstar, 1951. **$45.00 – 65.00**.

Golden Girl cleaning set in box is also by Norstar. It has a broom, dustpan, apron, and sweeper, c. 1964. **$45.00 – 75.00**.

### ***Susy Goose — "Toys That Mold Character"***

Kiddie Brush & Toy Company of Jonesville, Michigan, produced a line of toys known by the brand name Susy Goose. These toys were popular from the mid-1930s to the late 1960s.

The company, founded in 1930 by Paul A. Jones, Sr. and John Doty, was located in Bryan, Ohio. In 1932, Mr. Jones became sole owner and moved the company to Jonesville, Michigan. Shortly afterward, the name Susy Goose was born.

Susy Goose was the trademark for many different toys before the girl with goose was designed. For instance, in the early 1940s, the litho carpet sweeper in a cleaning set featured a mother pig dressed in an apron using the sweeper as a puppy looked on. The sweeper and other accessories were packed in a Susy Goose gift box. Soon, Susy riding the goose was developed by a female artist using the pen name Peter Maybe.

Kiddie Brush produced a variety of toys and was licensed by Mattel to use the name Barbie® on four-poster beds, vanities, wardrobes, and pianos. Ken wardrobes were produced, as well as beds, vanities, and wardrobes for Skipper.

By the mid-1960s "almost all steel stampings and twisted wire brush were gone and everything [was] plastics." Mr. Paul Jones, Jr. states: "All Susy Goose toys carried an owner's guarantee that if not satisfied in any way, return it, and we'll fix it or replace it." Mr. Jones further adds: "For the first few years of my career with Kiddie Brush, SERVICE was my responsibility. I can swear that every letter, toy received, I answered with a letter personally. 100% was answered!" Kiddie Brush Toy Company can be recognized as a company that stood firm in effort and principle to produce a quality product.

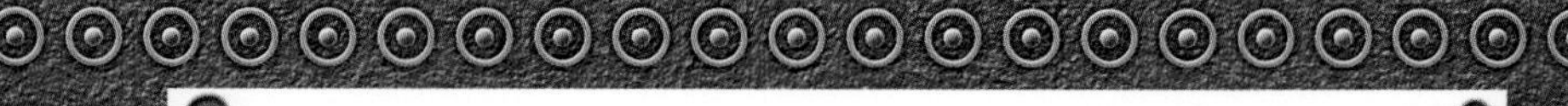



The earliest Susy Goose sweeper has a red background sprinkled with stars, and a jingle:

"With my sweeper
Work is fun
I'm a comin'
On the run!"

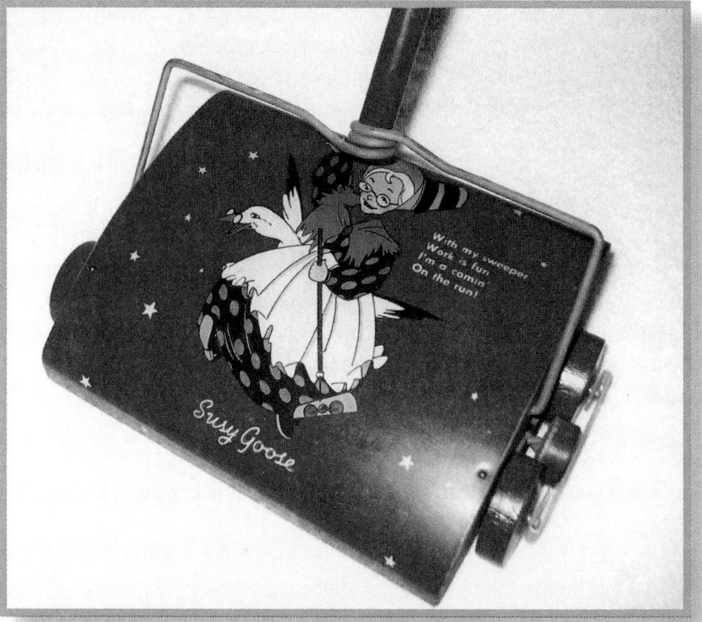


Susy has a goose flying behind her but she is walking with a sweeper in her hand. The company name, "Kiddie Brush & Toy Co., Jonesville, Mich., USA," appears in the lower right-hand side. The handle is 24" long. Later handles were reduced to 18". **$35.00 – 45.00**.

Probably the first Susy Goose cleaning set with the litho of Susy riding the goose became available in the mid-1940s. The sweeper surface was red with a triangular black inset featuring Susy Goose. At a distance, the goose is difficult to recognize because her wings, tail, and neck are dark gray, which provides little contrast against the black background. Kiddie Brush & Toy Co., c. 1945. Sweeper handle, 24" long. Broom, 30" long. Brush, 7¼" long. Dustpan by Wyandotte.
Pieces shown, **$75.00 – 125.00.**

The next design was a rectangular black inset with Susy Goose. The wings, tail, and neck of the goose are a lighter gray. The name of the artist, Peter Maybe, appears on this set. Kiddie Brush & Toy Co., c. 1950. Sweeper handle, 18" long. Broom, 27" long. Dustpan, triangular with wire handle. Pieces shown, **$75.00 – 100.00**.

In 1950, Spiegel showed the set with red and white dustpan, 27" broom, dustmop, duster, and plastic apron. The sweeper had changed to a round black insert with Susy Goose, and cobwebs had been added to the sweeper.

Reprint from 1950 Spiegel catalog.

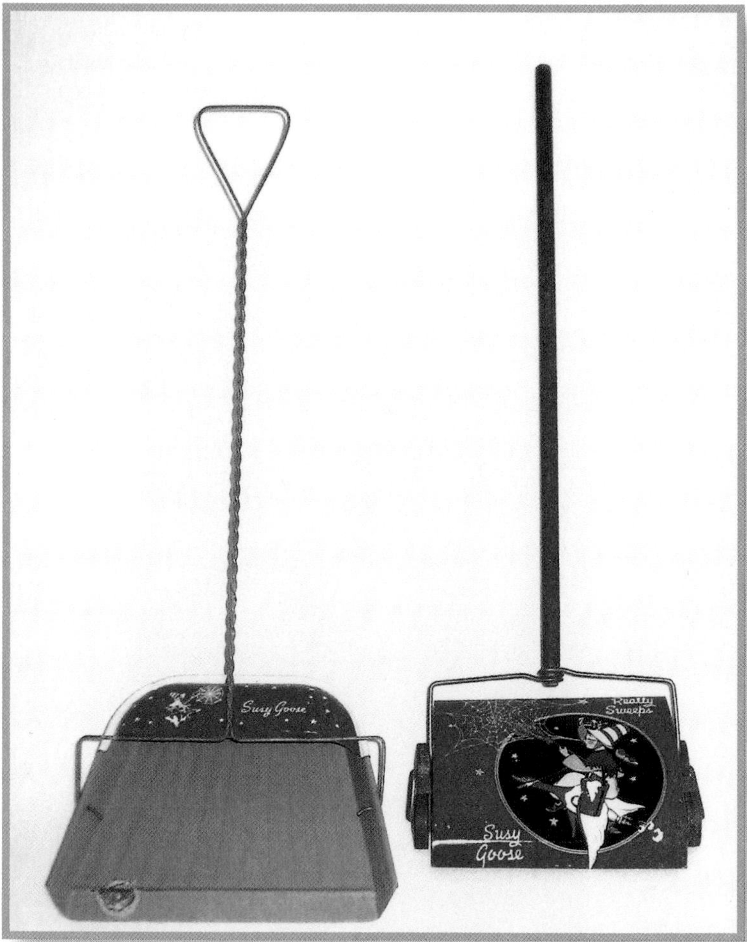

By the early 1950s, a new dustpan was designed, depicting the same cobwebs as those shown on the sweeper. The black inset was round. Kiddie Brush & Toy Co., c. 1950s. Sweeper handle, 18" long. Dustpan, hooded with wire handle. Pieces shown, **$55.00 – 75.00**.

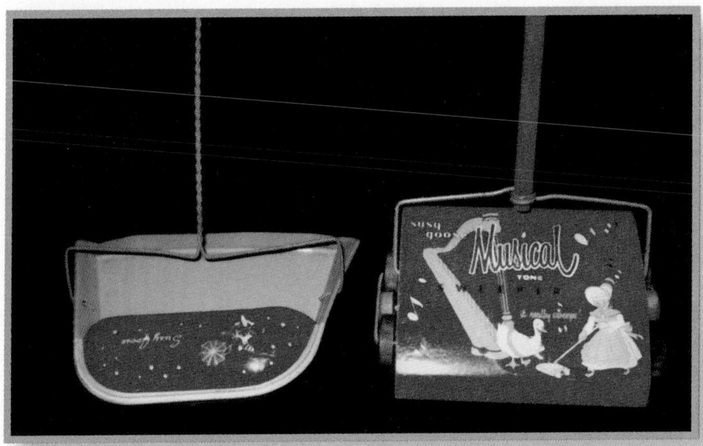


Musical Tone Sweeper by Kiddie Brush features Susy Goose sweeping the carpet. A happy duck backs up to a classical harp. The musical sound is a plink, plank, not a melody. Written on the underside is the Kiddie Brush guarantee: "This Susy Goose toy is guaranteed to please. If it isn't completely satisfactory please return and we'll repair or replace and pay transportation both ways. THE SIMPLE TASKS MOLD CHARACTER." The dustpan was found with the sweeper and has the same colors but may or may not have been with it in a set.

Sweeper and dustpan, **$55.00 – 75.00.**

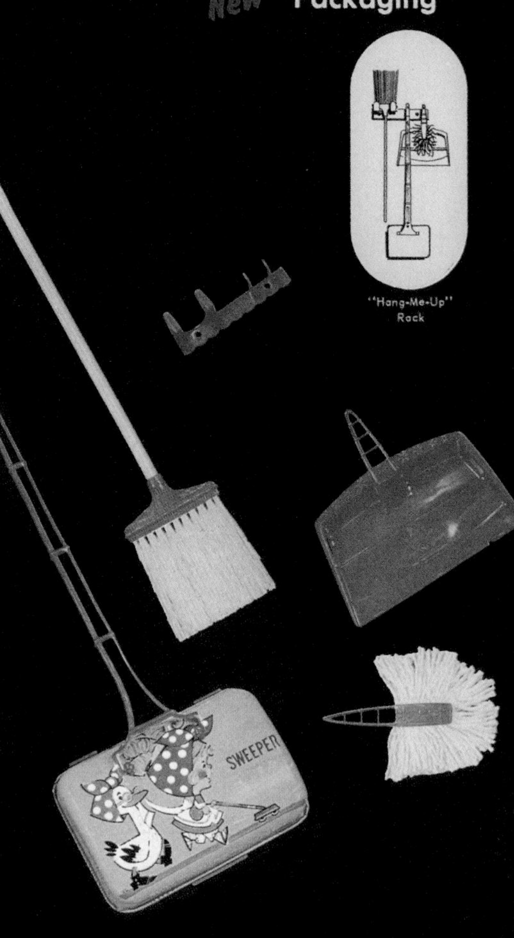

No. 132
NEW SUSY GOOSE HOUSEKEEPING SET.
New metal Sweeper. Sweeps – dumps. Box Size 23 x 8½ x 2. Overall wrap & shrink. Packed 12, Wt. 14 lbs.

Susy Goose catalog, 1967.

Susy Goose catalog (1967) featuring Mattel's Barbie® furniture.

In the early 1950s, Wolverine produced an attractive cleaning set described as "an entire home cleaning outfit including real step-on can, 7½" high inner container, waste basket, angle dust brush, dust pan in sturdy metal attractively decorated." The scene was Dutch blue and white. Wolverine set with wastebasket, Thalhimers' 1953 catalog.

**TC-16B—STEP-ON CAN SET by Wolverine. An entire home cleaning outfit including real step-on can, 7½ in. high, inner container, waste basket, angle dust brush, dust pan in sturdy metal attractively decorated..................2.98**

Five-piece Wolverine cleaning set, c. 1953. **$125.00 – 175.00**.

Wolverine also produced a cleaning set without a wastebasket. No. 268 features a dustpan, step-on can with insert, dustmop, and broom, c. 1953. Complete boxed set, **$175.00 – 225.00**.

# Wash Day

In the early Colonial period washing garments was done about once a month or after enough laundry had accumulated to warrant setting up for the dreaded task. Wooden tubs, washboards, soap made from ashes, grease and lye, a boiling pot, brushes, drying rack, bushes, clothesline, and clothespins completed the necessary equipment.

All types of devices to improve equipment for wash day were tried in Europe in the early nineteenth century. An early example of a washing machine was a wooden box with a crank. Clothes were placed in the box with appropriate water and cleaning element, and a crank turned the box over and over. It was an exhausting operation because the crank had to be turned by hand.

An early drier consisted of a pierced metal drum with a crank. It was held over a fire and rotated by the crank. If the fire was too hot, clothes could be burned. Often ashes and soot from the fire ruined the laundry. This drying machine never replaced the clothesline.

In the early 1900s, many average households were doing laundry in the kitchen, on the back porch, in an outer shed, or outside. If done outside, fire set under a cast-iron washpot heated water for soaking, scrubbing, and rinsing. If done in the kitchen, a wash boiler was used along with hot water from the cookstove reservoir. In upper-class homes, wash day was centralized in the basement.

Laundering toys give record of what was really used in households. These toys were often exact copies of the real thing. Davis Brothers' 1879 – 1880 catalog advertised a five-piece toy wash set consisting of metal washboard, wooden washtub, cedar pails, drying rack, and brush. Carl P. Stirn's 1893 catalog offered the same combination, but listed a folding table, which was an ironing board.

## *Early Wash Day Toys*

In the late nineteenth and early twentieth centuries, wash day toys consisted mainly of a wooden tub, wringer, washboard, and dryer, the folding type. Morton E. Converse and Son was a great supplier of laundry toys into the 1920s.

Wooden tub with tin bands and all-wooden washboard and wringer with a vertical bar that fits outside the tub rather than clamping on the side. Attributed to Converse, 1900. Tub, 5" in diameter. Washboard, 4½" x 2½". Wringer, 5¾" x 4¾". Tub and board, **$35.00 – 50.00**. Wringer, **$30.00 – 45.00**.

Tub and wringer were shown in Butler Brothers' 1914 catalog as separate items. The tub is natural wood with tin bands, 11" in diameter. The wringer is listed as: "Toy Wringer. Made by American Wringer Co., 7" x 6" wood frame, galvanize clamps, solid rubber rolls, strong springs, detachable handle." The wooden frame has black lettering: "American Wringer Co. New York." c. 1912 – 1919. Tub, **$35.00 – 65.00**. Wringer, **$75.00 – 100.00**.

Prior to 1920, many washboards were personalized with names like Star, Baby, First Lesson, ABC, Laundry Aid, etc. Dandy washboard, American, **$30.00 – 45.00**.

Wooden drying rack, 12" tall, American, 1915. **$35.00**.

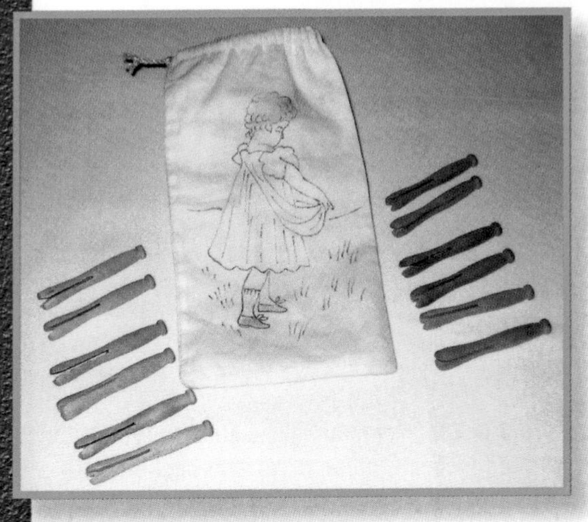

Clothespin bags became popular in the early 1900s. This muslin drawstring bag is stenciled "Dolly's Clothes Pin Bag" on the back and a little girl on the front. Bag has 12 original clothespins. **$25.00 – 40.00**.

Nearly a half century later, plastic clothespins and nylon lines were popular. This card marked "Copyright, 1958, Hoflion, Made in USA." **$25.00**.

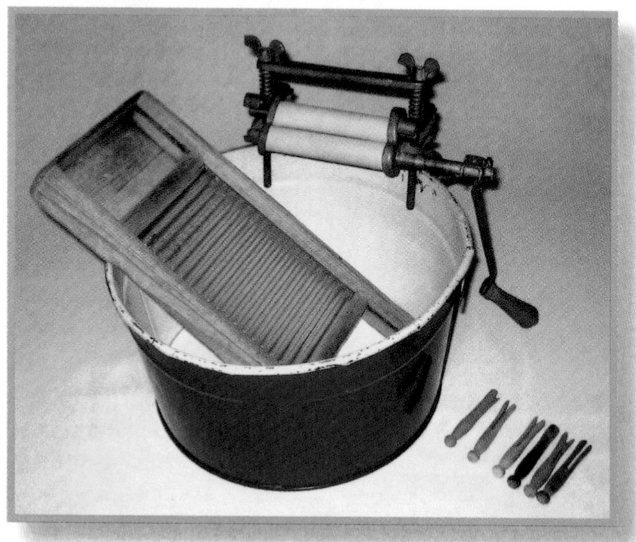

Blue and white 10" tub, wringer, 3¾", "crystal" glass surface washboard, 11" x 5⅛", and six clothespins. Clothes dryer and basket are missing from set. Wolverine, c. 1926. Pieces shown, **$65.00 – 100.00**.

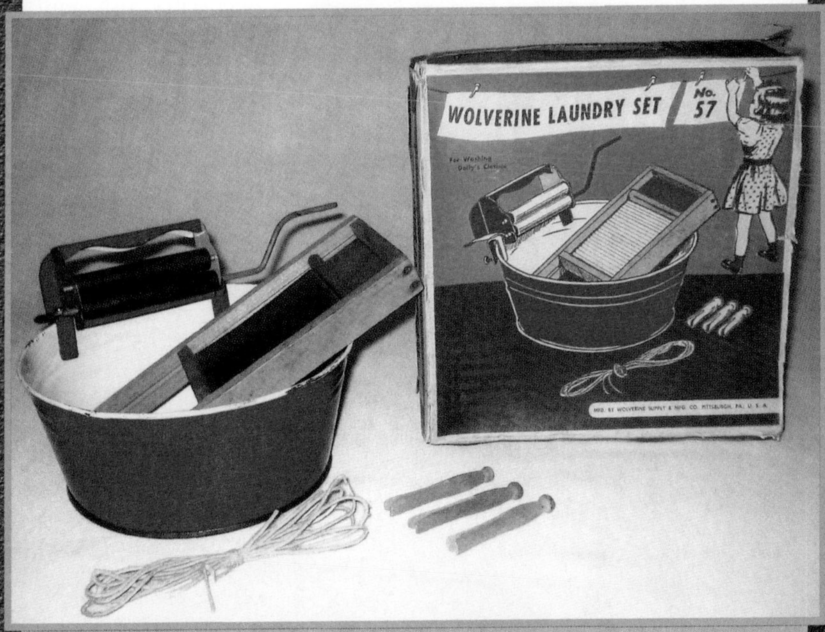


No. 57 set has tub, 6⅞" x 2¾", washboard, 7¼" x 3½", wringer, and three clothespins. Wolverine, c. 1940. Boxed set, unused, **$125.00**.

J. Chein & Company produced some very desirable wash day toys. This tub and washboard bear the early mark, the Chein name enclosed in a circle. Tub, 7" in diameter, washboard, pink enamel, 6½" x 3½", c. 1930s. **$55.00 – 95.00**.

No. 36 Laundry Set in box has same tub as No. 123 but inside is red enamel, washboard is pink. The graphics on the box are the same on the tub. Chein, tub 7" in diameter, washboard, 6½" x 3½", dryer, 9½" tall, six clothespins, c. 1930s. Boxed set, unused, **$250.00**.

Oval washtub is unique. The graphics depict two little girls busy with wash day. A puppy and mother hen with chick look on. Chein, tub 7¾" x 3⅛", c. 1960. **$25.00 – 45.00**.

This laundry set appeared in Spiegel's 1964 catalog. Tub, 7" in diameter, 3½" deep, washboard 7¼" x 3⅝", dryer 9½" tall, and iron. Basket and ironing board are missing. Wolverine. Pieces shown, **$65.00 – 85.00**.

6

She'll have
the cleanest
wash in town!

7 pc. set 2.97

6 LAUNDRY SET includes: wash tub, steel folding ironing board(16 in. high), play iron, steel washboard, revolving dryer, wicker basket.
Z36 J 5919. Clothes pins, too. Mail. (5 lbs)...Set 2.97

Spiegel 1964 catalog reprint.

## *Toy Washing Machines*

Toy washing machines were on the market by the early twentieth century. They were miniature examples of the real ones in households. In 1912, Converse featured a crude washer, "A copy of the real thing." It was 15" tall with a 10" tub on wooden legs. It was one of the first washers to appear in retail catalogs. By the 1920s, Chein, Ohio Art, Hoge, Wolverine, and others were sharing the marketplace. A new line of Sunny Suzy washers by Wolverine was well represented in retail catalogs and department stores.

Sunny Suzy washer No. 68 offered with or without accessories. Washer, 8¾" in height, 6⅞" in diameter. Wolverine, 1930s. **$55.00 – 75.00**.

In 1940, Wolverine's Blue Delph scene began its reign. The 1942 catalog showcases: "Washing machines with new decoration." It was offered individually or in a set. Wolverine, No. 79, 10¾" high, c. 1940s. **$75.00 – 95.00**.

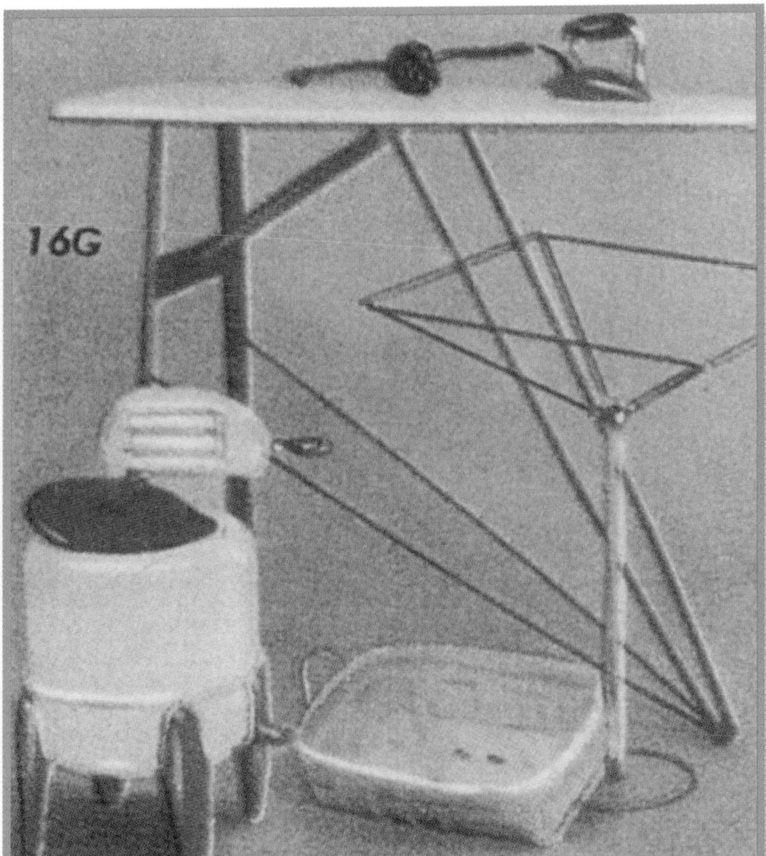

16G

**TC-16G—WASH-DAY SET** by Wolverine. Looks and works just like mother's. Underwriters approved electric iron, washing machine truly washes and wrings, large steel ironing board, clothes dryer, etc.................................. **6.98**

Thalhimers' 1953 catalog reprint.

Washing machine set listed in Wolverine's 1942 catalog and still being sold in 1948. Complete with 9" high revolving clothes reel, washer, 9" high, tub, 2¾" x 6⅞", and four clothespins (not shown). Wolverine, 1940s, set shown, **$175.00 – 225.00**.

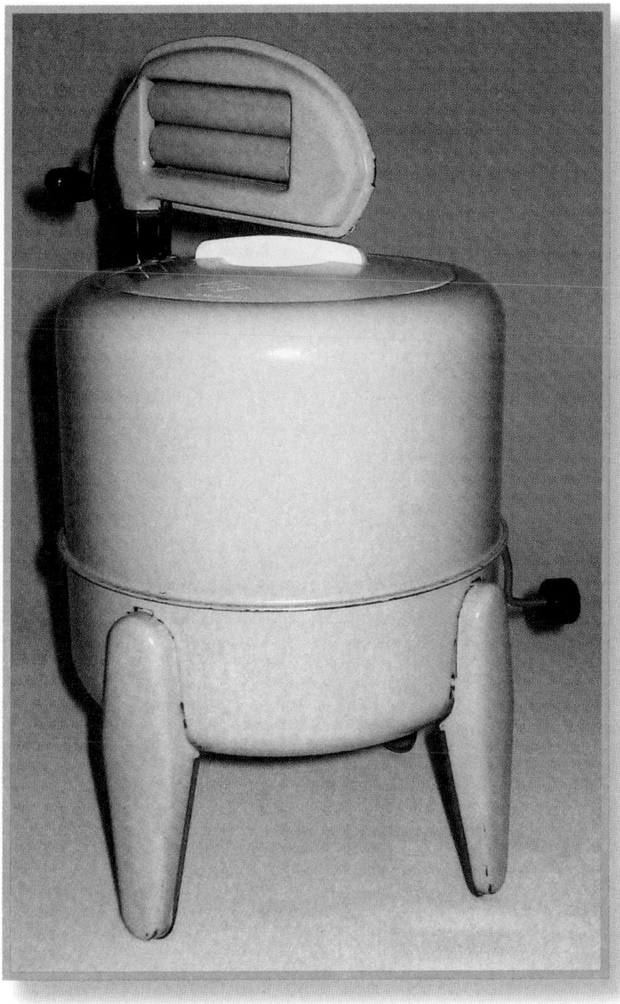

A new-style washer appeared in 1950. It was successful for a decade, produced in white enamel with red trim and in the favorite color, pink. Wolverine, washer 12" high, c. 1950s. **$75.00 – 95.00**.

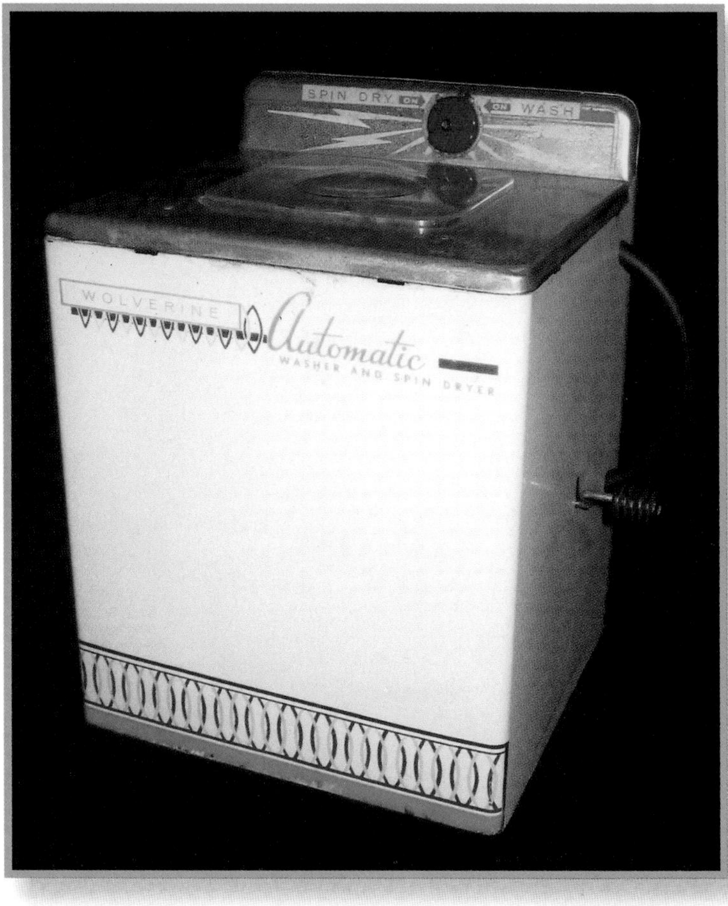

Automatic Washer & Spin Dryer was very popular, appearing in Wards' 1959, Sears' 1962, Spiegel's 1964, and Wolverine's 1968 catalogs . Washer-dryer, 8" x 7½" x 10½", 1950s – 1960s. Wolverine. **$55.00 – 95.00**.

Dolly's Washer,
Chein, c. 1930s.
**$100.00 – 125.00**.

Wash day name-brand products available with toy laundry equipment, 1900 – 1970. **$8.00 – 15.00 each**.

## *Electric Toy Washers*

White enamel washer is heavy and in working condition. Observing it at first, one might think it to be a salesman's sample, but it couldn't be, because it has no wringer nor drain tube. The red stamped logo is worn away. However, the cord bears a label, "Made in USA." American, maker unknown, c. 1930. **$75.00 – 100.00**.

La Petite Dolly's Electric Washer is in near-mint condition with original box. The top is heavily chrome coated. No other attachments came with washer. A metal label advises "Do not use when empty." Empeeco Appliance Corp., Chicago, c. 1930. **$125.00 – 175.00**.

## *Ironing Boards*

Table "bords" were brought to America with some settlers. They were flat boards that could rest on trestles or be placed on any sturdy structure. They served as eating tables, ironing tables, and in a variety of ways as space savers; placed out of the way, precious space was preserved. The colonists "made-do" for ironing and pressing, but by the late nineteenth century the ironing board as we know it today was becoming a necessity in American households.

Stenciled and painted ironing board depicts a little girl sitting on a bench at the bottom. The shape of the board reveals its early age. Early ironing boards were square at both ends. Later, they were tapered at one end. Converse, board 11¾" long, 7" high, 1900. **$35.00 – 65.00**.

American, makers unknown. Large board, 24" long, 16½" high, c. 1915, **$30.00 – 45.00**. Small board, 17" long, 14½" high, c. 1930, **$25.00 – 35.00**.

Converse, Newton & Thompson, and N.D. Cass were some of the companies producing wooden ironing boards into the 1950s. Toy wooden ironing boards were vanishing by the mid-1950s. Spiegel (1950) showed only one, and other catalogs were advertising the new steel ones. Wolverine was forefront in supplying enameled ones in solid colors and ones with litho scenes.

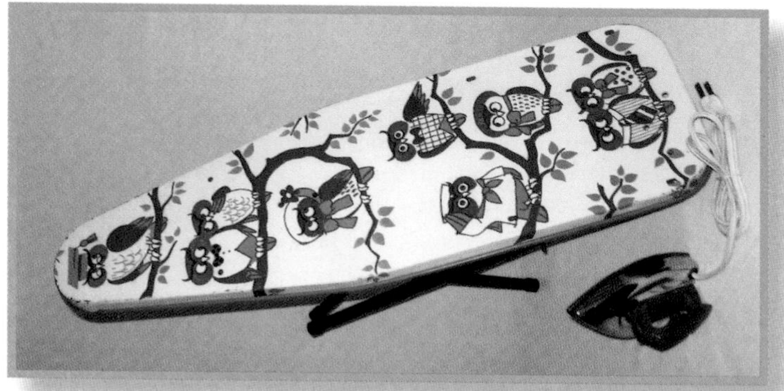

This board with perching owls (each wearing a different outfit) was made in 1968, Wolverine Toy Co., Pittsburgh. A subsequent one was produced c. 1970 with the Wolverine-Spang logo. **$55.00 – 75.00**.

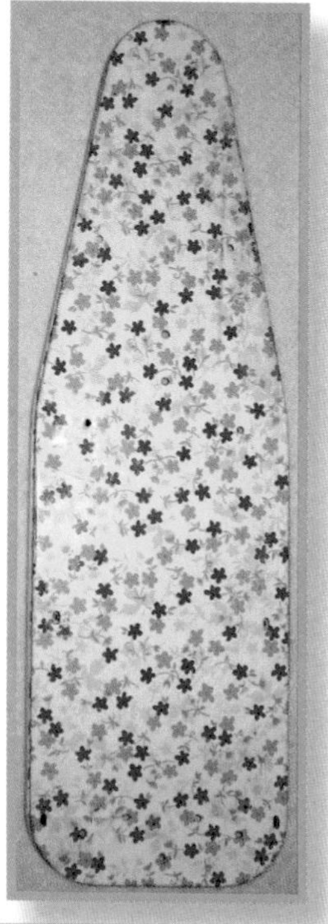

Floral ironing board. Wolverine, c. 1960. **$25.00 – 35.00**.

Sunny Suzy bears the Wolverine-Spang logo, c. 1970. Has matching iron. **$45.00 – 65.00**.

### *Irons*

Another implement very much used in the nineteenth and early twentieth centuries was the sad iron, or flat iron. Many affluent households had separate laundry quarters, but in the average American household sad irons were still heated on the kitchen stove, even as late as the 1930s. Toy sad irons were offered by Kenton, Hubley, Arcade, Dover, J. & E. Stevens, and others.

Prior to the 1880s, the handles of adult irons were heated with the plate. In 1871, Mrs. Mary Florence Potts of Ottumwa, Ohio, patented a sad iron with a removable handle. The handle was detached while the iron was heated and re-attached for ironing. The handle never got hot. It was a revolutionary breakthrough in the improvement of irons. Toy companies capitalized on the popularity of this new iron.

Left: Dover sad iron No. 602, 1900. **$35.00 – 65.00**.

Center: Kenton, Mrs. Potts-style on stand, c. 1920s. **$45.00 – 75.00**.

Right: Kenton, all cast-iron, on stand, 1930. **$35.00 – 65.00**.

Little Sweetheart Ironing Set No. 295 is unique with six clothespins, clothesline, and a small metal iron (3¾") made especially for this set. On the back is a cutout of doll and clothes. Wolverine, 1948. Boxed set, unused, **$55.00 – 75.00**.

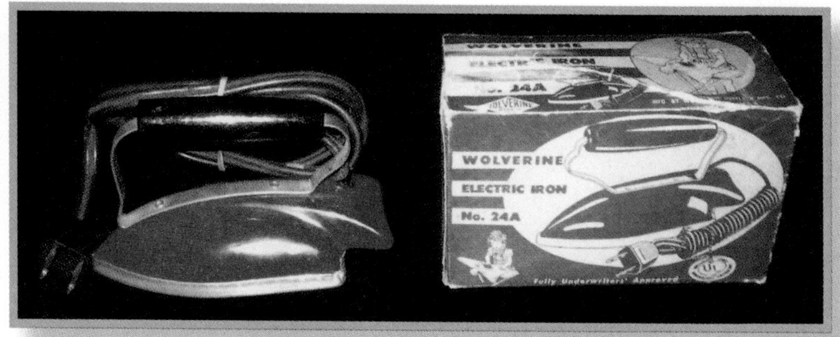


No. 24A Wolverine electric iron with box, 1940, **$65.00 – 95.00**.

No. 25A Wolverine electric iron with box, 1940, **$65.00 – 95.00**.

The word "mangle" was used in early times to describe an ironer for pressing flat items, such as bed linens. Hotels and laundries needed this type. In the 1920s, the ironer was listed in Sears for household use.

Mangle, 7" x 7" x 2½", c. 1930. The cover is flannel material featuring children with toys and animals. Maker unknown, but looks like Girard or Wyandotte. **$75.00**.

# Metal Tableware

Up until America entered World War I in 1917, most tin tea sets came from Germany. The war heightened loyalty toward "Made in USA," allowing American toy companies to gain a foothold. By 1918, Ohio Art Company was producing tin tea sets and companies like Chein, Wolverine, and others were poised for production.

***Ohio Art Tin Tea Sets***

The founder of Ohio Art Company, Henry S. Winzeler, was born in Archbold, Ohio, in 1879 and began his company determined to add artistic meaning to Ohio Art toys. He engaged highly qualified artists and allowed them artistic freedom. Some of the most popular artists, Fern Bisel Peat, Elaine Ends Hileman, Beatrice Benjamin, and others were allowed to initial or sign their designs. This elevated the artist to a position other than employee and some worked for the company a decade or more. Ohio Art is acknowledged as producing some of the most beautiful lithographed toys in the world.

### *GIRL IN SWING*

This set is said to be the first tea set produced by Ohio Art, c. 1918 – 1920s. It came with a large round tray, cups, plates (saucers), and teapot with lid. It is designed very much like the old German tin litho tea sets. The saucers have no cup ring and look more like plates.

Round tray, 6", **$100.00**.
Plate, 3½", **$75.00**.
Cup, 2", **$50.00**.
Teapot and lid, **$100.00**.
5-piece set, **$325.00**.
7-piece set, **$450.00**.

In 1921, Butler Brothers offered three Kittens sets: 6-piece, 12-piece, and 20-piece. Each set contained a 6¼" plate, 2⅞" saucer, 4¼" plate, and 2¼" teapot with lid. These sizes differed from the Girl in Swing set.

| GIRL IN SWING | KITTENS |
|---|---|
| *Lg. Plate, 6¼"* | *Lg. Plate, 6¼"* |
| *Sm. Plate, 3½"* | *Saucer, 2¾"* |
| *Cup, 2"* | *Cup, 1½"* |
| *Teapot & lid, 2¾"* | *Teapot & lid, 2¼"* |

***KITTENS***

5-piece set, **$175.00 – 210.00**.

In 1927, Sears' popular Santa Claus Stocking included an eleven-piece Kittens set containing three each, cups, saucers, and plates, and a teapot with lid. The price of the stocking was $1.98.

**_BLUE DELPH_**

This popular set came in several different sizes, from a five-piece Hummer set to a 20-piece set. 5-piece set, c. 1930s, **$100.00 – 125.00.** 7-piece set, **$150.00 – 175.00.**

A short time after production of the Girl in Swing set, the teapot and lid, 3½" plate, and 2" cup were discontinued. However, the tray continued on with other sets comprised of 6¼" tray, 4¼" plate, 2¾"saucer, 1⅞" diameter cup, and 2¼" teapot. The following sets contain this arrangement:

*BLUEBIRDS AND BLOSSOMS*, shown in Sears, 1924.
*MOTHER GOOSE*, c. 1930s.
*LITTLE RED RIDING HOOD*, c. 1930s.
*BO PEEP*, 1930s, listed in Sears, 1931.
*BUTTERFLIES*, 1930, listed in Sears, 1930.
*KITTENS*, 1920s.

*Note: Although appearing in Ohio Art catalog (1928), this set was produced earlier. It was shown in Sears (1924). The large tray was issued with a bird on a branch above a nest with eggs.*

***BLUEBIRDS AND BLOSSOMS***

Tray, 6¼"
Plate, 4¼"
Saucer, 2¾"
Cup, 1½"
Teapot and lid, 2¼"
15-piece set, **$200.00 – 250.00**.

### *MICKEY MOUSE HELPMATES*

Signed "Walt Disney," c. 1933. These sets came with round trays as well as rectangular trays. Some were trimmed in orange, some in red.

**Plate**: Mickey and Minnie doing dishes.

**Cup**: Mickey at table serving Minnie, Horace Horsecollar, and Clarabelle the cow.

**Saucer**: Mickey and Minnie dancing.

**Teapot**: Mickey on stage with hat and cane; Minnie playing the piano.

**Tray**: Mickey and Minnie boating as Pluto howls from the shore.

9-piece set, **$300.00 – 450.00**.

### *DONALD AND FRIENDS*

The plate features one of Mickey's nephews sneaking into the picnic basket. Clara Cluck cackles at Donald's tantrum. The cup offers a gathering of Mickey, two nephews, Clara Cluck, Donald, and Pluto. Both pieces are marked "Ohio Art U.S.A., W.D. Ent." c. 1930s, Plate, **$30.00**. Cup, **$35.00**.

Although this set is well represented in Kerr's Ohio Art book, many are unaware that this set features Mickey's two nephews (wearing caps an long shirts). The large tray features only Clara Cluck, Donald, and Mickey's two nephews. Mickey is on the cup.

### *THREE LITTLE PIGS*

Signed "Walt Disney, Ent." c. 1935 – 1939. The characters, colors, and detailed scenes makes this a very desirable set. The scene on the cup reveals the creative talent of Disney artists. After the wolf is done away with, the threesome gathers to celebrate. One is playing the piano, while the other two join in with flute and violin. On the wall is a portrait denoted as "MOTHER," a brood sow suckling six piglets. 15-piece set, **$275.00 – 325.00**.

The late 1930s and early 1940s brought on new pieces in large tea sets. Ohio Art described the very small plates as "butter plates" and the covered cake plate as "handled dish with cover."

## *DONALD DUCK*

Signed "Walt Disney Productions." This Donald Duck set possibly came in a 28- or 31-piece set. Years ago, when I was organizing my tea sets, I cast aside the damaged pieces. This tea set was very large, and I kept only 12 pieces: two plates, two cups and saucers, two butter plates, teapot with lid, top to cake plate, and tray. This set has been in my family for decades, and I don't remember a creamer or sugar, but I remember the cake plate and other pieces. 1939 – 1942, 12 pieces, **$175.00 – 225.00**.

***BUSY SQUIRREL***

This set is not frequently seen. The theme and rich colors afford it much interest. These pieces came from a 31-piece set. c. 1938 – 1940, ten pieces as shown, **$65.00 – 95.00**.

***PUPPIES***

This set is not easily found. It came with a tray. c. 1940s, 31-piece set, **$175.00 – 275.00**.

***SILHOUETTE***

This set came in three different sizes, 9-piece, 14-piece and 23-piece. This 9-piece set is missing the tray. c. 1937. Pieces shown, **$65.00 – 95.00**.

Cover of *Children's Play Mate* magazine designed by Fern Bisel Peat, August 1951.

Fern Bisel Peat was a talented, successful artist. She illustrated numerous children's books and paper doll sets and designed an impressive variety of toys for Ohio Art. From 1933 – 1953, she was art director for *Children's Play Mate* magazine. After World War II, the government designed a program to help rehabilitate emotionally wounded soldiers. Mrs. Peat was a vital figure in helping to conduct this program through art therapy.

Following are some tea sets designed by Fern Bisel Peat for Ohio Art.

***NURSERY RHYMES***

Plate, "Jack Be Nimble."
Cup, "Tom, Tom, the Piper's Son,"
Teapot, "Bo Peep."
9-piece set, c. 1940s. **$125.00 – 150.00**.

### *RAG DOLLS*

No. 21. These little characters have feet sewn like rag dolls. Sewn hands and feet are prevalent in Peat's designs. Each piece is numbered "21" and signed "Fern Bisel Peat." c. 1940. Plate, **$25.00**. Saucer, **$10.00**.

### *HUMPTY DUMPTY*

This set came with straight-sided cups and teapot with lid. Kresge's catalog, c. 1940 features Humpty Dumpty with round cups and round teapot describing it as "Gray check metal with yellow bird singing. Plates, saucers and cups for four and a tray and covered teapot are included." c. 1939 – 1940s. 9-piece set, **$100.00 – 125.00**.

**_BUNNY BIRTHDAY_**

This set was released in numbers in the mid- to late 1940s. It came in a seven-piece set with plate as tray and in a nine-piece set with 5" x 7" tray. c. 1940s. 7-piece boxed set, **$150.00 – 200.00**.

***TOMMY TUCKER*** plates came with a Bo Peep tea set and with the following set featured in *The Ohio Art Company: A Corporate History 1908 – 1983.* Both sets were designed by Fern Bisel Peat. Plate, **$20.00**.

CHILDREN'S TEA SET

No. 263-A, 23 piece Tea Set, 1938

Tommy Tucker and Bo Peep tea set.

Fern Bisel Peat's illustration of *The Night Before Christmas.*

Elaine Ends worked under the directorship of Peat at *Children's Play Mate* magazine before she became Elaine Ends Hileman. Hileman's illustrations of children are exceptional. Her voluptuous little creatures have exaggerated feet and legs. Her animals are always happy and poised for play. Hileman certainly understood children to render such expression and movement in these little tykes.

***CIRCUS***

c. 1948, 21-piece set, **$175.00 – 225.00.**

Illustration by Elaine Ends Hileman from *Children's Play Mate* magazine, August 1951.

### *SHE LOVES ME, LOVES ME NOT*

Nine-piece boxed set, Ohio Art, artist, Elaine Ends Hileman, c. 1948 – 1950s. 9-piece set. This set is signed. Look at the plate and find the name "Elaine." **$125.00 – 150.00**.

LEMONADE AND COOKIE SALE

Have the cookies packed in small wax-paper bags.

Have the lemonade ice-cold and keep it covered at all times. It is better to bring a fresh pitcher from the house every little while than to make a lot at one time. Large quantities may become watery or warm before they can be sold.

Serve it in paper cups kept clean under a sheet of wax-paper.

You may serve peanut-butter sandwiches, also. Pack them in wax-paper bags. And serve peanut-butter *only*, as other kinds may spoil quickly on a hot day.

Illustration by Elaine Ends Hileman from *Children's Play Mate* magazine, August 1951.

***DUCKY BATH TIMES*** set is complete with teapot, creamer, sugar, plates, cups, saucers, and butter pats. Designed by Elaine Ends Hileman, c. 1940s. 31-piece set, **$175.00 – 250.00**.

***FLORAL SET*** is complete with teapot, creamer, sugar, plates, cups, cake plate with cover, and butter pats. 31-piece set, c. 1940. **$125.00 – 150.00**.

Another artist, Beatrice H.K. Benjamin, designed beautiful toys for Ohio Art. In addition to tea sets, Peat, Hileman, and Benjamin tackled any art design Ohio Art needed. Tops, pails, pumps, washing machines, and other toys are records of their talents.

***MEXICAN BOY***
c. 1940. Artist, Beatrice H.K. Benjamin. 15-piece set, **$125.00 – 175.00**.

### *GIRLS AS KITTENS*

Although this set is attributed to Fern Bisel Peat, it may have been designed by Beatrice Benjamin. Observe the faces in "Mexican Boy" and "Queen of Hearts," both designed by Benjamin. They closely resemble the faces in "Girls as Kittens." c. 1940s. 31-piece set, **$175.00 – 250.00**.

***QUEEN OF HEARTS*** tray by Benjamin, c. 1942. **$30.00**.

***BOY AND GIRL IN GARDEN***

This set first came with oval aluminum handles and round teapot with lid. Later, in 1956, the cup handles were straight across, and the teapot was straight-sided with no lid. 15-piece set, c. 1950, **$100.00 – 125.00**. 14-piece set, 1956, **$85.00 – 115.00**.

### *BLUE WILLOW*

Produced from the early fifties through the late fifties, this set is early, indicated by the round teapot. A straight-sided creamer is missing. 21-piece set, c. 1950. **$125.00 – 150.00**.

By 1955, the Blue Willow set featured the tall teapot instead of the round, bulbous one.

**_BLUE HEAVEN_**

This set was produced from the late fifties into the sixties. The sugar and plastic pitcher are missing. c. 1957. 21-piece set, **$100.00 – 125.00**.

**_BLUE HEAVEN_** was featured in Ward's 1959 catalog with creamer, sugar, and water pitcher. Catalog reprint.

**Metal Dish Set** (shown above). Colorful and inexpensive—designed for the toddler set. Even the youngest tots love to have their own dinner and tea parties for their friends and doll families. Pieces have smooth rolled edges and are nicely lithographed in attractive "Blue Heaven" design.

**Service for Four Includes:** Serving Tray (8x10 in.), 4 each of cups, saucers, dinner plates, butter plates, a sugar bowl and creamer, plus plastic water pitcher. Gift Box.

48 T 4634—Service for 4 (20 pcs.). Ship. wt. 1 lb. 8 oz. . . . . 98c

***SWISS MISS***

This set came in the Luncheon Service box labeled "Miss Petite." In 1965, Ohio Art named the pink set with blue poodles "Miss Petite"; same set could be renamed after some lapse of time. For example, in 1961, No. 414 was labeled "Dixie Bell;" this same set, No. 414, was offered again in 1965 as "Colonial Charm." This re-naming occurred in other examples; Swiss Miss" was probably named "Miss Petite" in the early 1950s. c. 1950. 20-piece boxed set, **$100.00 – 125.00**.

It's Such Fun to Entertain Our Guests

(H) 28-PC. "SWISS MISS" TEA SET. Service for 6. It's time for a party! What a thrill to cook her own refreshments (see food mixes sold on opposite page) and serve friends on her own set of dishes.

Dishes are metal charmingly lithographed in bright "Swiss" colors blue, green and red. Smooth rolled edges. Set includes 6 each plates, butter plates, cups and saucers; teapot, sugar bowl, creamer and an [illegible]x10-in. tray that helps little girls learn to serve graciously. Plates 4⅛-in. [illegible]am.; other pieces in proportion. For "silverware" to use with "Swiss [illegible]" Tea Set, see (T) below.

[illegible]1664—28-Pc. Set. Ship. wt. 1 lb. 8 oz............Service for 6 98¢

Swiss Miss came in a tea set also. Ward's 1957 catalog featured the tea set. Catalog reprint.

***BLUE BIRDS*** was featured in Ohio Art's 1956 catalog. It came in an eight-piece set with tray, two cups, two saucers, two plates, and a straight-sided teapot with no lid. 8-piece set, **$55.00 – 85.00**.

***APPLE AND PEAR***

This set came with a round teapot and lid. Another set came with an open teapot (on far right). The set with round teapot is early 1950s. 14-piece set, **$75.00 – 95.00**.

***LEAVES***

In 1962, this set came as a breakfast set. The cup handles were litho metal. Later, it was produced with aluminum handles. Tray, **$25.00**. Cup, **$10.00**.

***DIXIE BELLE***

Known also as Colonial Charm, this No. 414 set was produced in pink and peach colors. No teapot, creamer, or sugar came with this design. c. 1960s, 17-piece set, **$75.00 – 95.00**.

**_GOOD MORNING BREAKFAST SET_**

This set appears in the Ohio Art 1966 catalog. It sold in Western Auto's 1968 catalog for $3.99. Missing from this set are flatware, plastic creamer and sugar, and plastic fruit bowl. 1966. Complete set, **$100.00**.

**_SUNSHINE BREAKFAST SET_**

This has the Ohio Art 1972 – 1978 logo. It contains the hard-to-find plastic bowl with fruit. Ohio Art, c. 1972. Complete set, **$85.00**.

***HUMPTY DUMPTY***, 1970. 13-piece set, **$85.00.**

***OWL,*** 1980, six-piece set on card, **$45.00**.

***HAWAIIAN FLORAL,*** 1960s. 7-piece set, two cups, two saucers, two plates, and round tray. **$45.00**.

1908 - 1933
1934 - 1958
1908 1983
OHIO ART
The World of Toys™
Le Monde Des Jouets
El Mundo De Juguetes
Die Welt Des Spielzeugs
1959 - 1982
1983 -

Page from *The Ohio Art Company: A Corporate History, 1908 – 1983.*

### *Wolverine Tea Sets and Salad Sets*

Wolverine made four known tea sets: blue Delph; strawberry design; yellow and red set sprinkled with gold stars; and a floral one, Royal Dresden Rose. In this set, the teapot, creamer, and sugar are made on a different mold.

This blue Delph set came with a large tray, six cups, six saucers, six plates, teapot, creamer, and sugar. c. 1940s. It is shown in the company catalog (1942) as: "Sunny Suzy Dish Set No. 258. Decorated in Attractive Delph Blue Pattern." 22-piece boxed set, **$175.00 – 225.00**.

Sunny Suzy, No. 258-S strawberry tea set came with six cups, six saucers, six plates, teapot, creamer, sugar, and tray. 22-piece boxed set, **$175.00 – 250.00**.

The Stars pieces have the same measurements as the blue Delph and strawberry sets. Wolverine, 1950s. 12-piece set, **$65.00 – 95.00**.

Spiegel in 1964 and Wolverine in 1968 advertised Fiesta Ware cook sets and salad sets. The salad set was comprised of a main bowl, four individual bowls, salt, pepper, salad fork and spoon, and flatware.

Fiesta Ware Salad Set. 7-piece set shown, **$45.00 – 65.00**.

Bo Peep was also available in the cook and salad sets. 7-piece set shown, **$45.00 – 65.00**.

Little Sweetheart Salad Set No. 253 dates to the 1950s. Each piece has the Wolverine logo and the fork and spoon are marked "MADE IN USA." Boxed set, **$65.00 – 95.00**.

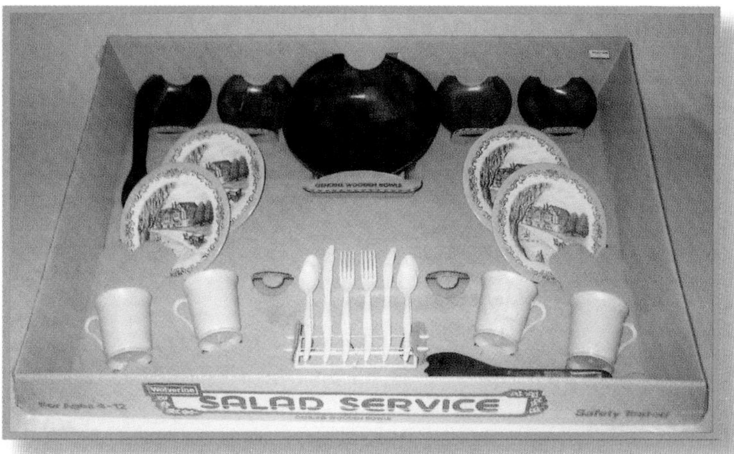


This Wolverine Salad Service has genuine wooden bowls, salad fork, and spoon. "Wood parts were made in Taiwan." Wolverine Toy, Division, Spang Industries, Inc., c. 1970. Boxed set, **$55.00 – 75.00**.

### *J. Chein & Company*

J. Chein & Company produced some early tea sets featuring Krazy Kat, Mickey Mouse, Donald Duck, and, in later years, Mary Poppins, Snow White, Holly Hobbie, Peanuts, and others. Many floral sets were also part of the company's tea set line. In the 1970s, the company became known as Chein Industries. The company discontinued toy production c. 1979.

Disneyland Tea Set featuring Mickey, Minnie, and Pluto. Walt Disney Productions, c. 1955. 7-piece boxed set, **$200.00 – 275.00**.

Krazy Kat, George Herriman created the comic strip character, Krazy Kat, c. 1913. Herriman was a cartoonist for Hearst newpapers, which continued the strip until the 1940s. J. Chein & Co., c. 1930. (Tri-colored shield.) Pieces shown, **$150.00 – 175.00**.

Bunnies was a popular set in the 1950s. 13-piece boxed set, **$100.00 – 125.00**.

Early American Play Time Tea Set, c. 1958. 13-piece boxed set, **$100.00 – 125.00**.

Candy Canes, c. 1960. Pieces shown, **$30.00 – 45.00**.

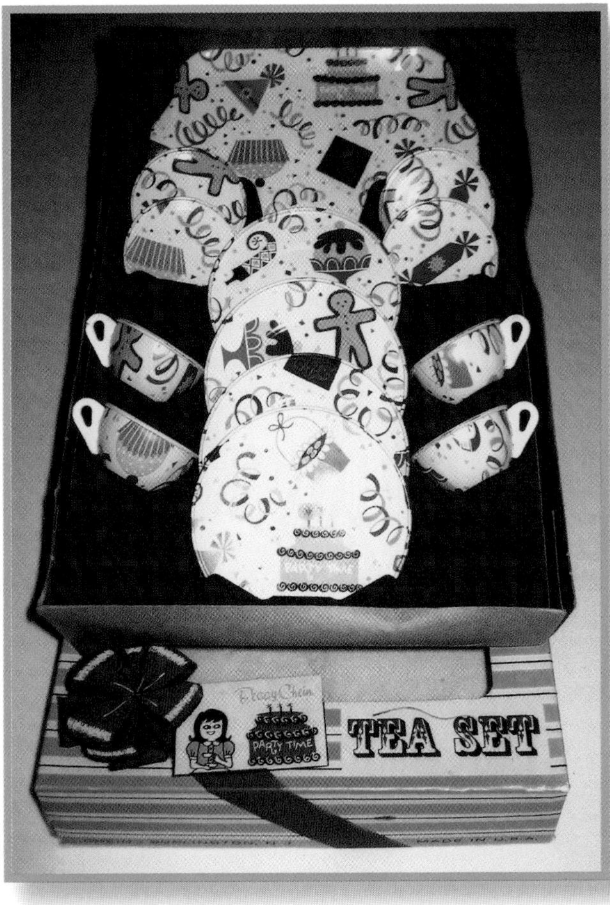

Birthday Party, c. 1955. 13-piece boxed set, **$100.00 – 125.00**.

Snow White, Walt Disney Productions, c. 1960. This set is mint without the box. Set contains 12 pieces of flatware, four each of cups, saucers, and plates, also a creamer, sugar, teapot with lid, and tray. 29-piece boxed set, **$150.00 – 175.00**.

Mary Poppins, Walt Disney Productions. Dated 1964. This set is mint without the box; same pieces as Snow White. 29-piece boxed set, **$150.00 – 175.00**.

Little Girls at Tea, No. 210. The box has an interesting cover with cutout faces of the girls. The scene is filled with flowers, bluebirds, and bright colors. Chein, c. 1950. Missing tray and teapot. 8-piece set in box, **$125.00 – 150.00.** Pieces shown with box, **$65.00 – 90.00**.

### *Aluminum Tea Sets*

The popularity of aluminum tea sets began in the early 1900s. By 1917, John Smyth catalog advertised 15 tea sets. Only two were aluminum. By 1912, Sears offered five different sets. By 1930, Sears was offering plain and fancy sets. The embossed sets with nursery rhyme characters were introduced in the early 1930s. Sears advises: "Now we are offering the expensive EMBOSSED DESIGN pieces at no increase in price." In the late thirties, a noticeable decline ensued as the war years loomed.

The 1950s brought on large, beautiful sets depicting favorite characters. Spiegel (1950) advertised: "43 piece embossed 'Bo Peep' set." Following were Three Kittens and Cinderella. Kiddykook, Aluminum Specialty Co., produced numerous sets in the fifties.

"Like Mother's" by Mirro Aluminum Company of Manitowoc, Wisconsin. The company is well-known for bake sets and tea sets. This Three Kittens set was a bestseller, c. 1950s. 27-piece boxed set, **$150.00 – 175.00**.

Character coffee and teapots by Mirro.
Left to right:
Cinderella dripolator, c. 1940.
Cinderella percolator, c. 1950s.
Bo Peep percolator, c. 1950s.
Three Kittens percolator, c. 1950s.
Three Kittens teapot, c. 1950 – 1960.
Each, **$18.00 – 25.00**.

Flatware by Mirro, c. 1950. 26-piece boxed set, each piece marked "MADE IN USA." **$35.00 – 55.00**.

### *Pewter or Britannia*

Other metal tea sets included pewter, later called Britannia. In the nineteenth century, porcelain and electroplating were strong competitors of pewter, forcing improvement in its quality. Pewter companies like Peter Pia, established in America in the late nineteenth century, improved the appearance of toy pewter with a silvery finish called Britannia. By the early twentieth century, the name "pewter" in toy metal had changed to "Britannia."

Butler Brothers in 1895 listed tea sets as "pewter," as did John Wannamaker in 1905. By 1917, however, John Smyth listed the same tea sets as "Britannia metal tea sets, silver finish." By the early 1900s, the word pewter had disappeared from advertisements.

This Britannia tea set could have been produced as late as the 1920s. 23-piece set, **$100.00 – 125.00**.

This set is older pewter (Britannia), c. 1900. These pieces are heavy with lead content. Using the edge of the little cup, the alphabet can be written on white paper. 23-piece set, **$100.00 – 125.00**.

This metal red apple has a small table and tea set hidden inside. It was made by Wyandotte, formerly known as All Metal Products Co., Wyandotte, Michigan. The table is lithoed, and the top features children — an Indian, cowboy, skater, and a child rolling a hoop — all popular themes in the 1920s – 1930s. The white metal tea set is very intricate, with tiny spoons. **$100.00**.

# Plastic Tableware

As the Depression years were winding down, plastic was making a quiet presence in industry. Several toy firms were already adding plastic parts to toys. Kilgore, noted for cast-iron toys, was using plastic in 1937. The giant Hubley was using plastic grips on its famous guns in 1941, and many other firms had turned to plastic by that time.

The appearance of plastics post-World War II was phenomenal. Expansive changes occurred in household and industrial areas once factories were tooled for this new material.

Advantages over other materials were numerous. Plastic provided finer details in the product. Labor costs and shipping costs were lower, and it was deemed safer than glass. Being lightweight, it afforded better manipulation for little hands. Toy companies eagerly embraced this "cure-all" product.

The years 1938 – 1958 laid groundwork for American plastics to acquire a major position in industry. Many fine toy companies developed and added respectable contributions.

With all its benefits, many parents and buyers were skeptical. The buying public was accustomed to wood, tin, glass, and cast-iron in toys. Items made of this flimsy material with strange colors were looked upon by many as "throw-aways." Some seemed to wait, thinking factories would get back to old goods. Plastic, however, was the result of a new idea with possibilities of great benefits, and it would never go away.

Spiegel 1950 catalog reprint.

***Banner Plastics Corp., New York, New York***

Banner Plastics produced an impressive array of tea sets and "crystal" beverage sets in the late 1940s. This clear stemware set was advertised in the Sears catalog (1948) as "Shining Stemware. Clear as glass, practically unbreakable plastic in a pretty floral pattern. Service for four – 4 sherbets, 4 goblets, water pitcher, and some colorful straws."

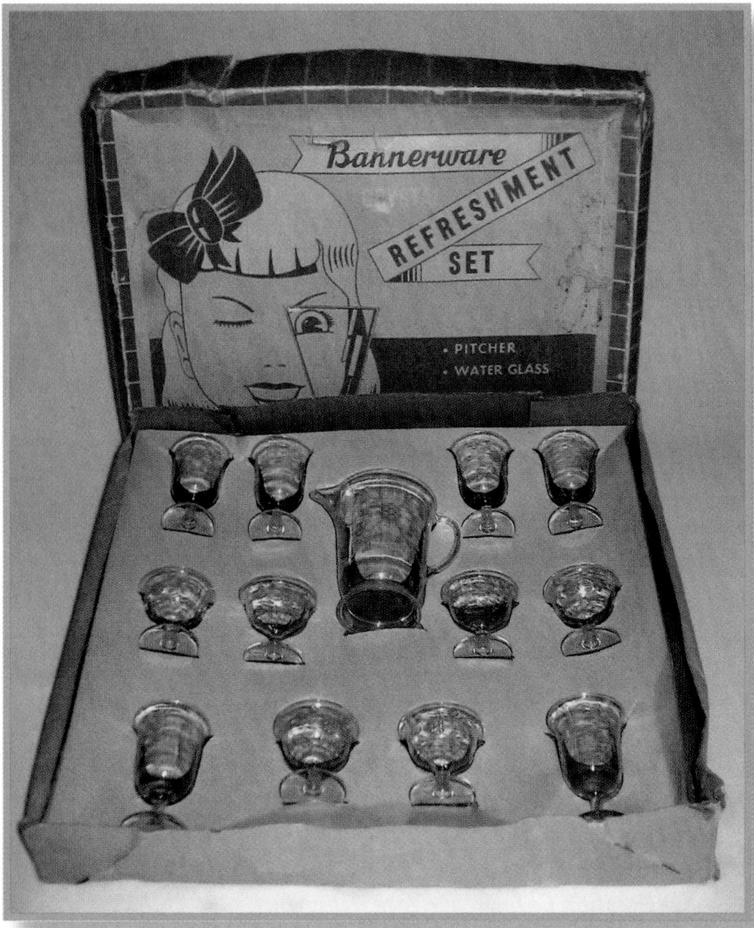

Bannerware Crystal Refreshment Set, c. 1945 – 1948. 13-piece boxed set, **$45.00 – 75.00**.

This Lazy Susan has been seen with crystal sherbets, goblets, and water pitcher in a tea set. Crystal with Lazy Susan, **$30.00 – 45.00**.

In the 1950s, Banner became very productive in all types of plastic tableware. Two of the company's most treasured sets came with litho metal dishes combined with plastic pieces. Alice came with litho and plastic, as did the Fantasy set shown below.

Fantasy Bannertone tea set, c. 1950. This set with lavender and blue tones is complete. The coffeepot has a trivet and the sugar has a lid. Other plastic pieces consist of cups, creamer, two sherbets, flatware, and covered tureen. Plates, saucers, and cereal dishes are litho metal. 37-piece boxed set, **$100.00 – 125.00**.

Pink Chocolate Set, c. 1950. This set is made of good, brittle plastic. It also came in iridescent silver. All pieces are marked "BANNER, USA." 9-piece set, **$30.00 – 45.00**.

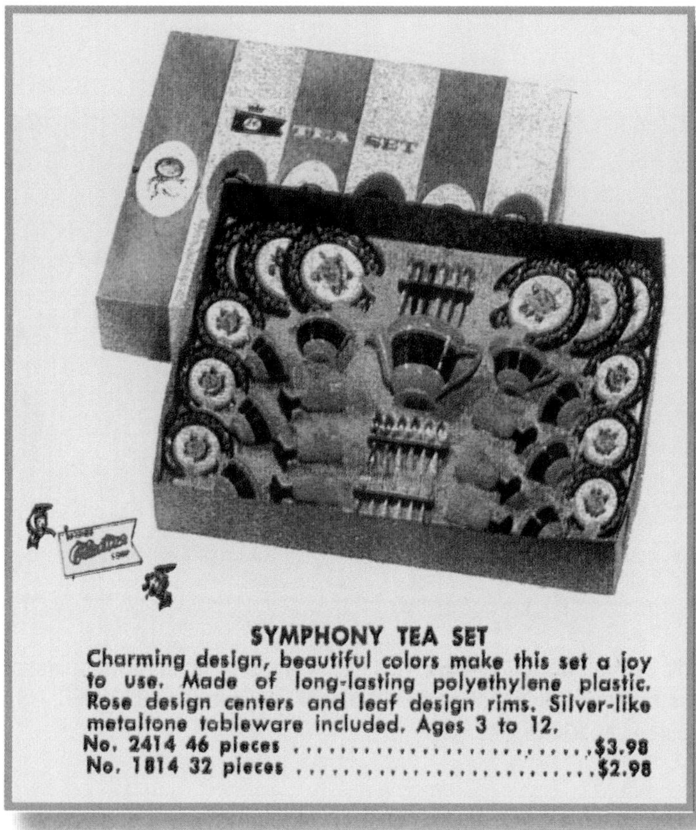


A later Banner tea set, Rucker-Rosenstock catalog, 1957.

### *PLASCO (Plastic Art Toy Corp.)*

This company made many interesting plastic tea sets. Four different Alice in Wonderland tea sets were produced. These sets were available from 1945 to the late 1950s.The company was located in Rutherford, New Jersey, and boxes are sometimes marked "Carlstadt, NJ" and "East Rutherford, NJ."

Alice In Wonderland PLASCO Tea-Time Dishes. This boxed set has a serving plate, cups, saucers, two small plates, and no teapot. The saucers have Queen of Hearts; the serving plate has the Mad Hatter; and DoDo bird is on the cups. The pieces have hand-painted floral designs, even on the flatware. The box is dated 1945. Shown also are oval plates and demitasse cups and saucers from a larger set. 13-piece set with good box, **$65.00 – 95.00.**

Alice pink transparent set has the same characters on the same pieces as described on page 235, c. 1945 – 1950. 7-piece boxed set, **$35.00 – 50.00**.

Alice in Wonderland by PLASCO, 1949. The characters on this set are applied white plastic, Alice on teapot, Frog on sugar, Rabbit on creamer. No plates were in this set; cups and saucers had no applied plastic. Flatware for two. 14-piece boxed set**, $75.00 – 100.00**.

This Alice set for four has applied white plastic on all pieces except saucers, which bear an embossed Queen of Hearts. It came with flatware for four. By PLASCO, 1949. 28-piece set, **$75.00 – 100.00**.

Worcester Ware tea set, c. 1950. This company made many beautiful plastic tea sets. The pieces featured are made of hard plastic. The plates measure 6" and the flatware measures 6¼". All pieces are marked "Worcester Ware." Seventeen pieces as shown, **$35.00 – 55.00**.

This blue and white Worcester set has never been removed from the box. "Mfg. By Worcester Toy Co., Worcester 5, Mass. Made in USA." c. 1950 – 1960. 26-piece boxed set, **$65.00 – 100.00**.

Another Worcester set, Rucker-Rosenstock catalog, 1957.

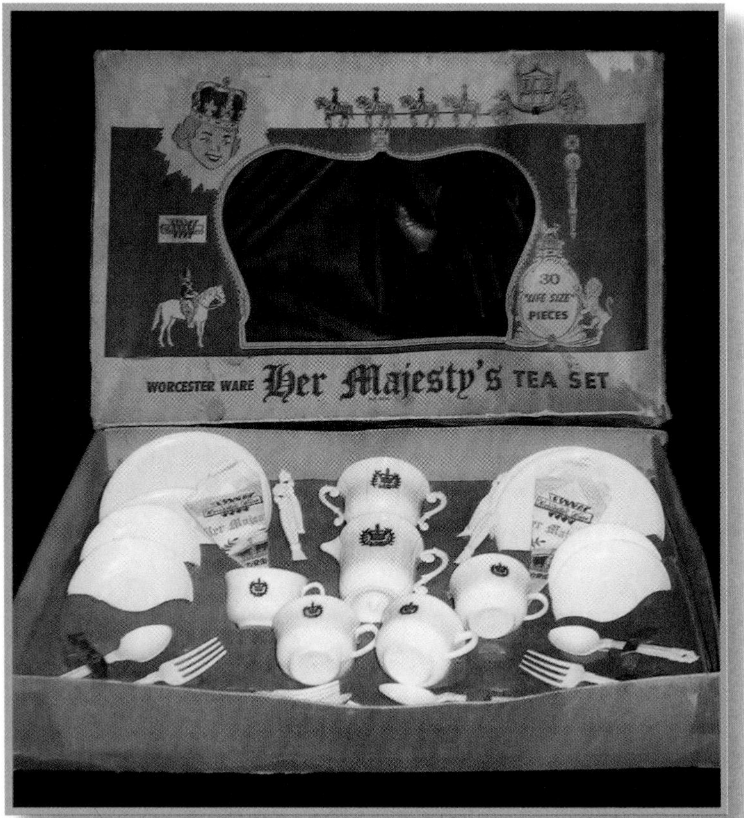

Her Majesty's Tea Set relates to the 1953 coronation of Elizabeth II of England. The plates and saucers are plain; cups, sugar, and teapot feature the crown. Worcester Ware, c. 1954. Boxed set, **$55.00 – 75.00**.

This Marx No. 2093 "Complete 44 Piece Plastic Tea Set" has 39 pieces. One fork and four napkins are missing. All remaining pieces are in excellent condition. One special item is the yellow plastic tablecloth, 26" x 20." The box is segmented inside. The pieces are marked: "Made in USA Marx." 44-piece boxed set, **$65.00 – 100.00**.

Ideal Beverage Set, c. 1950. The pieces are hard plastic. The tray has a hobnail bottom; water pitcher, goblets, and sherbets have a floral design. 6-piece set, **$35.00 – 50.00**.

### *Irwin Corporation*

The Irwin Corporation was in plastic production beginning with celluloid in the 1920s. Irwin Cohn is said to have pioneered production for "injection and blow molded" toys. Irwin produced its own plastic, which resulted in a cost-saving advantage. A huge number of tea sets and other toys came from the factory, well-made and colorful, establishing Irwin as one of the finest companies producing plastic toys.

Gay Victorian Dinner Set, c. 1950s. The box says "Large Dinner size pieces, beautifully executed by the finest designers. A proud possession to own." Also, "an extremely lovely filigree pattern, artistic and dainty to brighten your table with a richness unequal." Tea urn, 7½", plate, 6", saucer, 4", creamer, 2", sugar, 2", cup, 2". Complete 15-piece boxed set, **$75.00 – 125.00**.

Irwin Punch Bowl Set. Rucker-Rosenstock catalog, 1957.

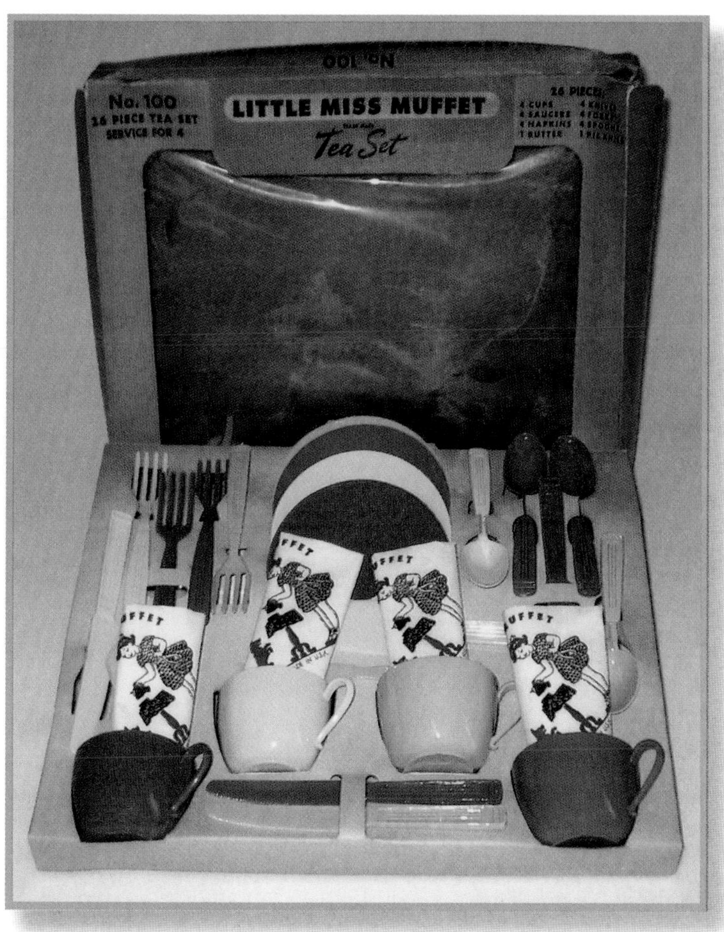


Little Miss Muffet Tea Set by Gotham Industries, Inc., New York and Chicago. This set is very attractive, and the pieces have never been removed form the box. "No. 100, 26 piece Tea Set Service for 4." 26-piece boxed set, **$75.00 – 100.00**.

Another "Little Miss Muffet" set by Gotham was produced in transparent colors. Featured in Rucker-Rosenstock 1957 catalog.

Kiddykook Tea Set. Among the many toy companies changing from metal to plastic, Chilton, Aluminum Specialty Company of Manitowoc, Wisconsin, trademark, "Kiddykook," fared well in the transition. Tea set complete with spoons, c. 1970s. All pieces marked with company name. 13-piece set, **$20.00 – 30.00**.

**IDEAL'S RUSSEL WRIGHT PLAY DISHES**

Make-believe homemakers, Mr. Wright has designed this modern dish set just for you. Teapot, sugar bowl, creamer, plates, cups, saucers, metalized knives, forks and spoons. High impact plastic. Ages 3 to 8.

No. 4628 ........................................ $2.98
No. 4627 Smaller Set ........................... $1.98

Reprint from Rucker-Rosenstock 1957 catalog.

***Russel Wright Dinnerware***

From the late 1930s, several American potteries produced dinnerware designed by the popular American designer Russel Wright. By the 1950s, Ideal Toy Company had secured rights to produce, in plastic, toy copies of Russel Wright dinnerware. The tea sets were "Modern in styling – just like the 'grown-up' set." This modern design combined with muted pottery colors was new to toy tea sets.

In 1957, Ward's advertised the set with pink teapot, creamer, and sugar, gray saucers, tan cups, and yellow plates. These colors continued to be mixed in various combinations.

By 1962, Sears advertised "Famous Russel Wright design," a tea and dinner set with platter, casserole with cover, and gravy boat with underplate. These sets are popular with collectors and prices continue to rise.

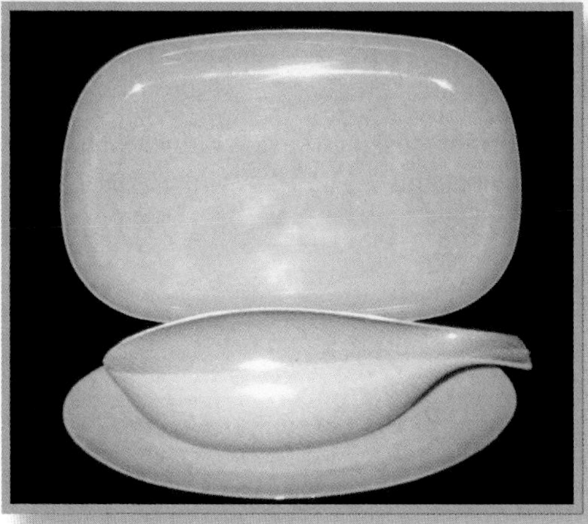

Dinner pieces. Platter and gravy boat with underplate, **$40.00**.

American Modern by designer Russel Wright. Made by Ideal, 1956. 23-piece tea set, includes 9-piece flatware, **$65.00 – 95.00**.

Refreshment Set by Ohio Art, c. 1960s. Metal tray, 3¾" x 5½", goblet, 2⅞", sherbet, 1⅜", boxed set, **$45.00 – 65.00**.

Bestmaid Children's Tableware, Made in U.S.A. c. 1950. 8-piece set on card, **$25.00**.

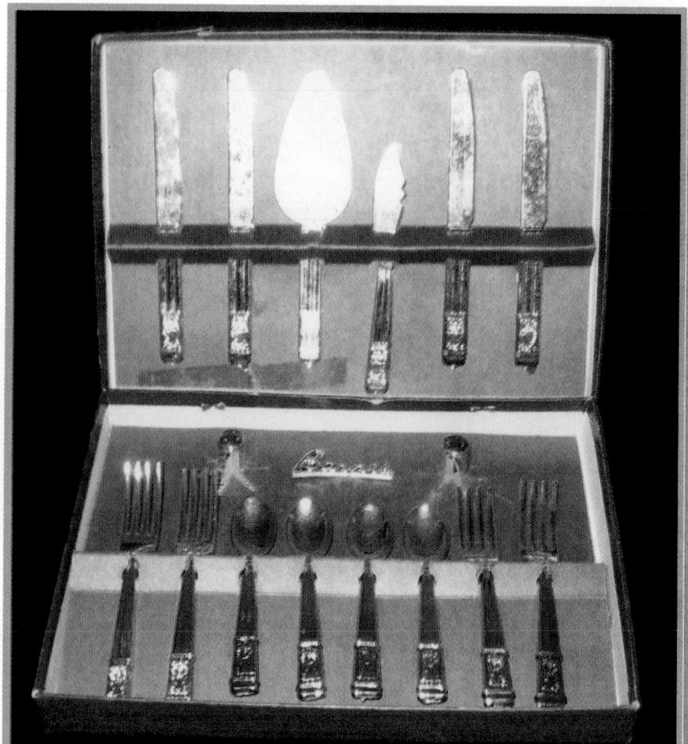

Banner Metal Tone, c. 1950. 16-piece boxed set, **$30.00 – 45.00.**

Florentine Tea Set. The scenes on the box feature Victorian children playing ring-around-the-rosy. The plates and saucers have a cutwork border. The urn has instructions: "Tea Urn with REAL Push Button SPOUT." 34-piece set, pieces marked "Irwin," c. 1950. Boxed set, unused, **$125.00 – 175.00**.

# MISCELLANEOUS

Arcade is noted for producing toy copies of full-size, name-brand kitchen furnishings such as Boone, Curtis, Crane, and others.

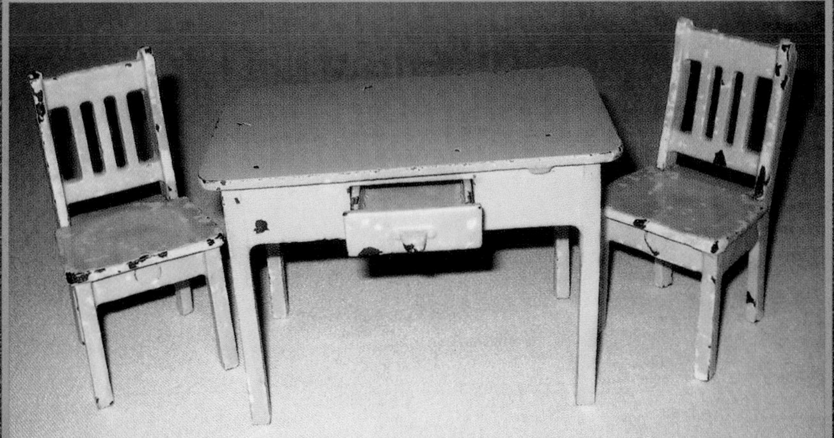

Arcade table and chairs. The pieces are miniature cast-iron copies of Boone models, c. 1920s – 1930s. 4-piece set, **$75.00 – 125.00**.

Alaska Ice Box has three hinged doors, two shelves on the right-hand side, and a block of ice. 7½" x 5¾" x 3½". Hubley Mfg. Co., 1920s. **$150.00 – 175.00.**

Faux electric refrigerator marked, "All Metal Products," an early name for Wyandotte. It measures 9½" x 3½," c. 1920s. **$75.00 – 125.00**.

**_Kilgore Mfg. Co._**

Kilgore Mfg. Co. of Westerville, Ohio, developed a toy business c. 1920s. The fine quality and low prices quickly established the success of the company. Cap pistols became major sellers and today are sought after by collectors. Fire engines, trucks, cars, airplanes, Sally Ann toys, and many others were unusually popular.

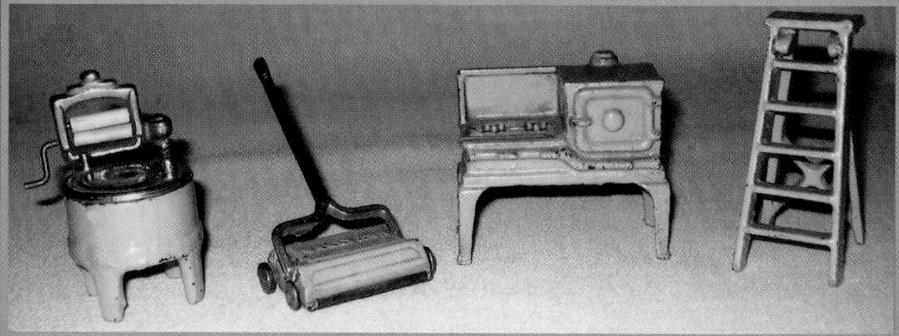

Butler Brothers advertised Sally Ann toys in 1930: "Sally Ann Household Set, aver. 2½" x 2", 5 pcs., sweeper, wringer, stove, washer, ladder," c. 1930. **$175.00 – 200.00**.

"Sally Ann Playground set, aver. 2½" x 2", 5 pcs., swing, teeter totter, kiddie car, stroller, slide," c. 1930. In red, **$175.00 – 225.00**.

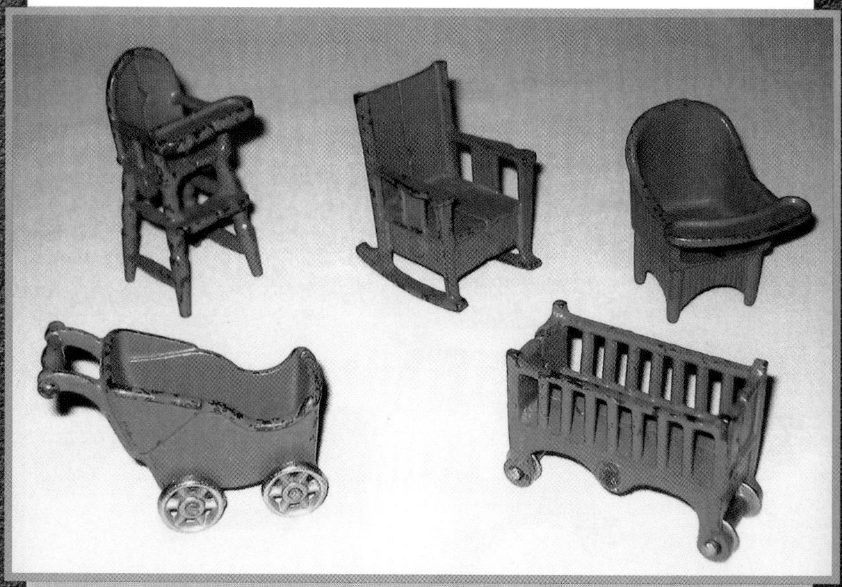

"Sally Ann Nursery Set, aver. 2¾" high, 5 pcs. Nursery (potty chair), rocking chair, high chair, carriage, bassinet," c. 1930. **$175.00 – 200.00**.

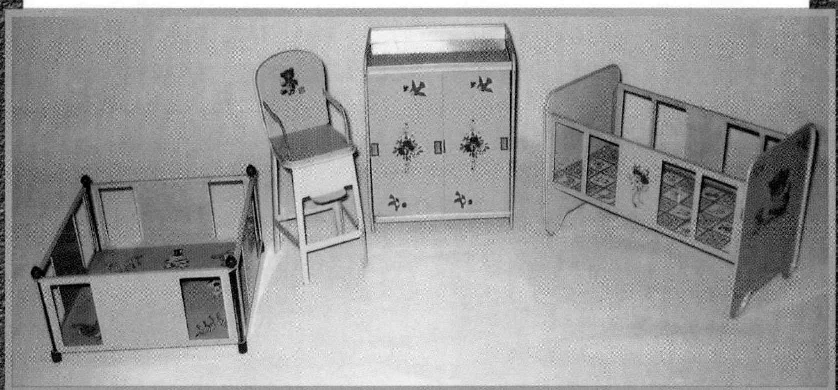

Four-piece furniture set, wardrobe, high chair, crib, and playpen, came as a set, by J. Chein & Co., c. 1956. **$125.00 – 150.00**.

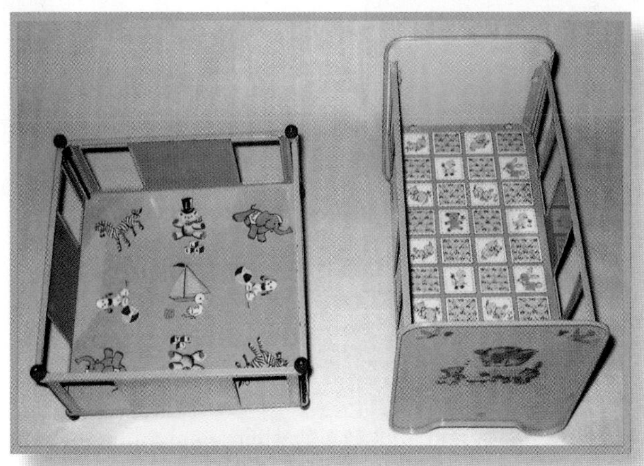

Close-up of crib and playpen.

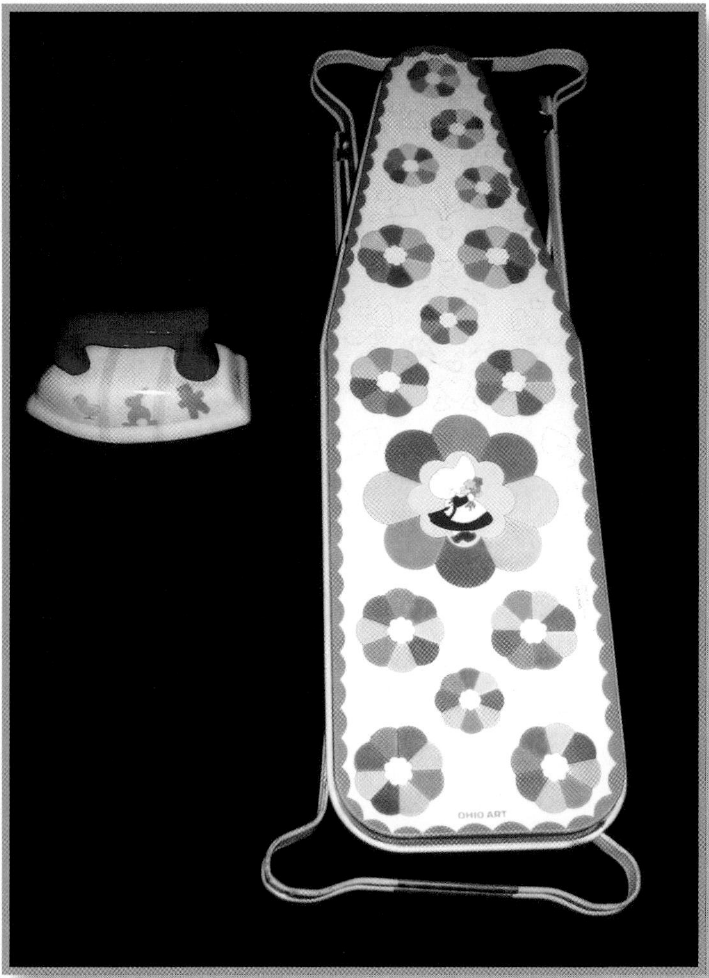

Ohio Art ironing board and iron. The little girl wears a bonnet and holds a bouquet of flowers, c. 1950. Board and iron, **$45.00 – 55.00**.

Little Lassie Clothes Line and Pin Set was advertised in *Life Magazine*, c. 1950. The clothesline is cotton, and the clothespins are wooden, some painted. Arandell Products Company, Philadelphia, Pennsylvania. Unused, **$20.00 – 25.00**.

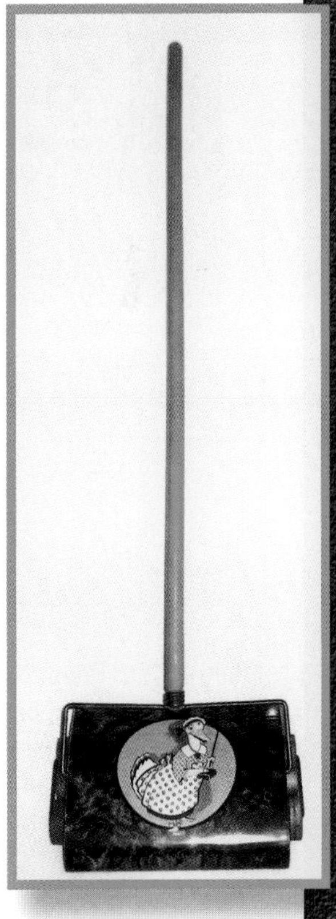

This sweeper may have been a 1960s model from Kiddie Brush, since the litho design is so similar to the 1942 sweeper. The early model featured a mother pig in a floral apron using a sweeper. This model with the goose holding the sweeper has the same apron design. **$35.00 – 45.00**.

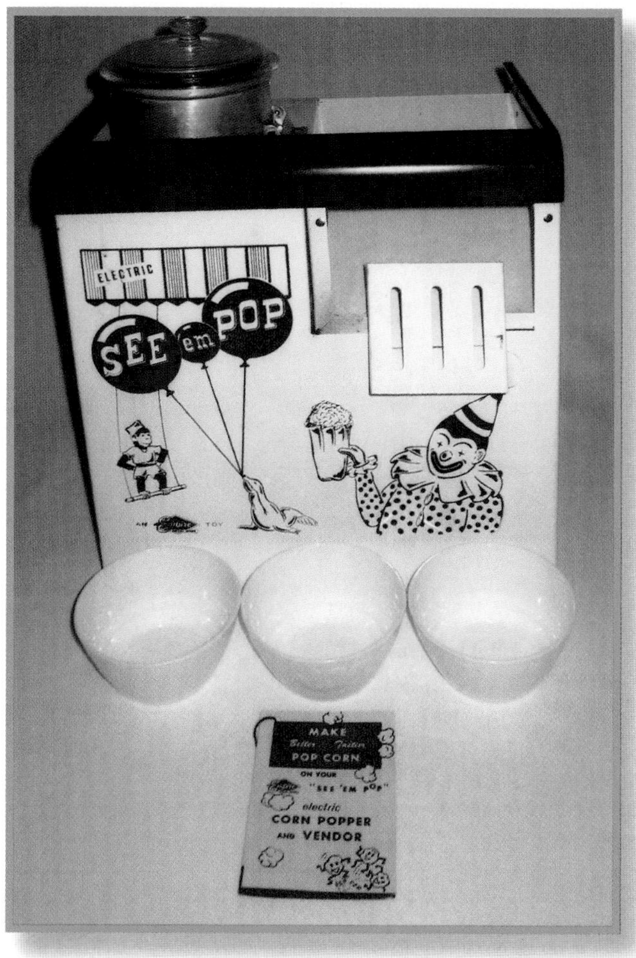


Electric Corn Popper and Vendor by Empire, the Metal Ware Corp., Two Rivers, Wisconsin, c. 1959. This was a popular item, featured in Ward's 1959 catalog, in white, with four plastic bowls. Sears (1962) advertised it with bags instead of bowls. In 1964, Spiegel featured it with four bowls. Complete with four bowls, **$100.00 – 125.00**.

"Little Deb" Lemonade Server Set. The metal trays were made by "Northwestern Products Co., St. Louis 3 MO US of A." The glasses and pitchers were provided by Hazel-Atlas. The set on the right was produced in 1946, the one on the left, c. 1950s. With box, **$75.00 – 100.00 each set.**

Close-up of trays.

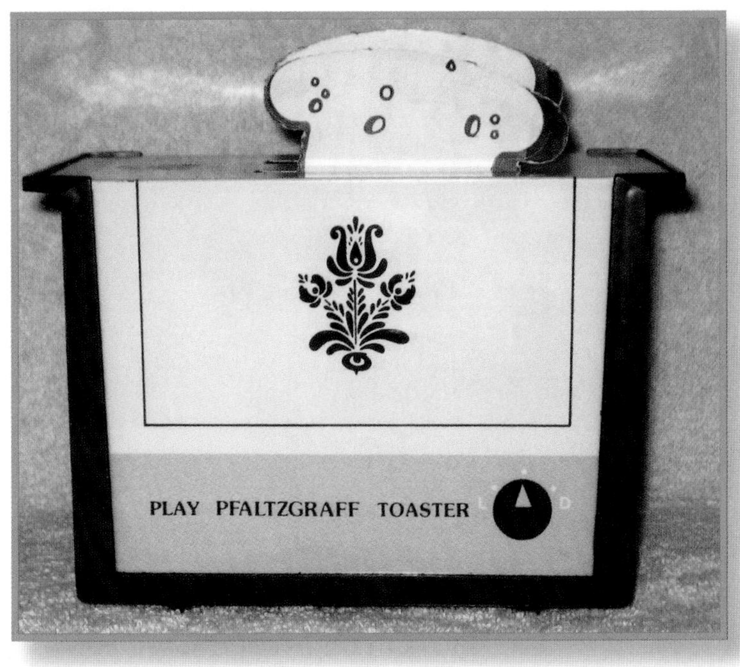


Play Pfaltzgraff Toaster, a mechanical toaster operated by a lever on the left side. Ohio Art Co., c. 1970s. **$15.00 – 25.00**.

No. 95 Doll House with 28 pieces plastic furniture, 1949

Reprint from *Ohio Art 75th Anniversary History, 1908 – 1983.*

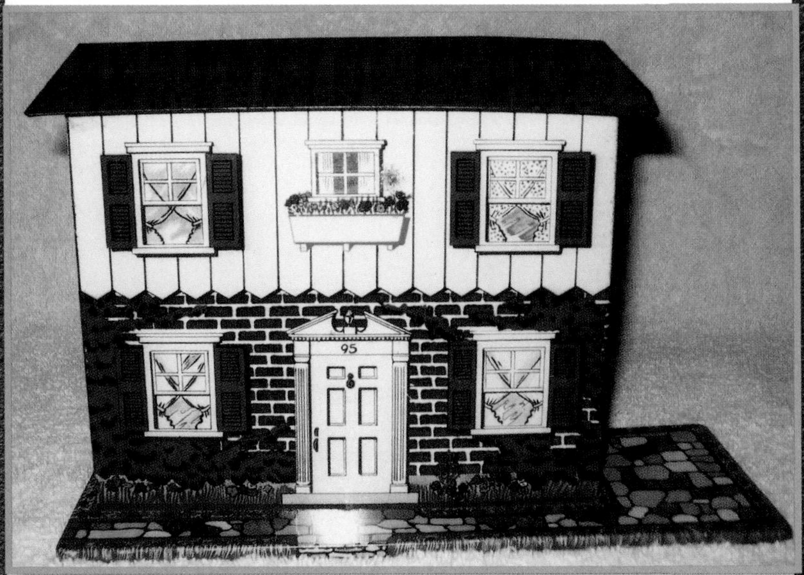


Ohio Art Doll House, exterior front view. Many are very surpised when they see the real doll house. It appears so much larger in toy books than it really is. It is being shown on the next page with an Ohio Art tea set tray to show its unusual size for a doll house. Measures 3" x 8½" x 5¼", 1949. Shown with Ohio Art Circus tray designed by Elaine Ends Hileman. Without furniture, **$65.00 – 95.00**.

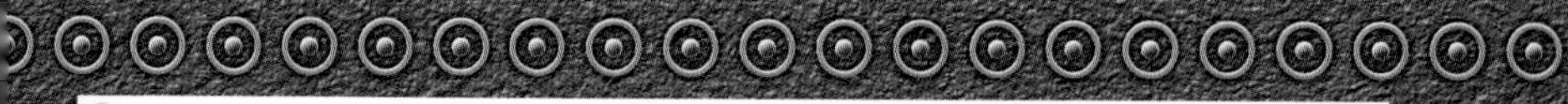

Interior back view.

Exterior front view with tray, both on same level.

German toy sewing machines are noted for artistic designs, classical lines, and beautiful, hand-painted motifs. American toy sewing machines, such as Singer and Gateway, are plain, without fancy additions, but appealing because of their strong, functional quality.

The Gateway sewing machine, c. 1930 – 1940, is made of heavy sheet steel and operates smoothly. 7" high. Gateway Company, Chicago, Illinois. **$65.00 – $95.00**.

The Singer sewing machine came with instruction book, clamp, and key. The box offers this information: "A SINGER FOR THE GIRLS. Teaches them to make clothes for their dolls. 'As the twig is bent, the tree's inclined.'" Singer Mfg. Co., New York City, 1922. **$85.00 – 115.00.**

E & L Mfg. Co., New York, used the title, "Johnny and Mary" in many toy sets. This Johnny and Mary Junior Kitchenette Set has an unusual combination. It offers lunch on a tablecloth with Plasco's "Alice" one-place setting. The dishes can be washed with Vel and Brillo using a DuPont sponge, then dried in the dish rack, c. 1950s. **$55.00 – 85.00**.

Country Kitchen, also called Farm Set, 1957. This set was purchased from a very reliable person who declared it came in the box without a tray. Ward's 1957 catalog confirmed what the person told me; this set was featured without a tray. The tray was not mentioned, nor counted in the number of pieces in the advertisement. It has the earmarks of a set in transition. The teapot finial is heavy chrome, which never appeared in other sets. The sugar has a lid with a heavy metal finial; sugar lids never appeared in other sets. Twenty-one pieces shown, no tray, sugar with lid, **$75.00 – 100.00**. 21-piece regular set with tray, no sugar lid, **$125.00 – 150.00**.

## *Betty & Bob*

Between 1960 and 1970, Lifetime Toys-Mfg. by Carolina Toycrafters, Charlotte, North Carolina, a division of Carolina Tool and Die Co., produced several Betty & Bob aluminum utensils. A label on each box identifies the utensil.

Left to right:

Chicken fryer, **$15.00 – 25.00**.
Serving trays, boxed set of two, **$15.00 – 20.00**.
Dutch oven, **$15.00 – 20.00**.

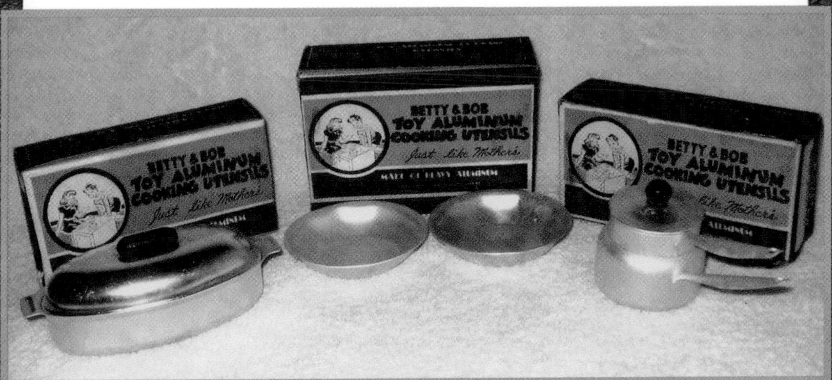


Left to right:

Roaster, **$20.00 – 30.00**.

Cake pans, boxed set of two, **$15.00 – 20.00**.

Double boiler, **$20.00 – 30.00**.

### ***Tupperware***

Earl Tupper began retailing his new invention, Tupperware polyethylene kitchenware, in the 1940s. By 1951, retail sales were discontinued, and all Tupper's energy was in the promotion of "Tupperware Home Parties." The company was very successful, and, c. 1958, Rexall Drug Co. (later Dart Drug) acquired Tupperware Company. Dart Industries is named on the box: "Tupperware, Orlando Florida 32802, 1979 Dart Industries Inc."

Tupperware Mini-Serve-It boxed set, **$45.00 – 65.00**.

# BIBLIOGRAPHY

Alexander, Brian S. *Spiffy Kitchen Collectibles*. Krause Publications: Iola, WI, 2003.

Asakawa, Gil and Leland Rucker. *The Toy Book*. Alfred A. Knopf: New York, 1992.

Daiken, Leslie. *Children's Toys Throughout the Ages*. Praeger: New York, 1953.

Earle, Alice Morse. *Home Life in Colonial Days, 1898*. Berkshire House Publishers: Lee, MA, 1993.

Florence, Gene. *The Collector's Encyclopedia of Akro-Agate Glassware*. Collector Books: Paducah, KY, 1975.

Ford, Dick and Joan. *Cast Iron Cook Stoves & Ranges*. Schiffer Publishing, Ltd.: Atglen, PA, 2003.

Grober, Karl. *Children's Toys of Bygone Days*. London: B. T. Batsford, Ltd., 1928.

Franklin, Linda Campbell. *From Hearth to Cookstove*. House of Collectibles: Orlando, FL, 1978.

Jacobs, Charles M. *Kenton Toys*. Schiffer Publishing, Ltd.: Atglen, PA, 1996.

Jaffe, Alan. *J. Chein & Co*. Schiffer Publishing, Ltd.: Atglen, PA, 1996.

Kerr, Lisa. *American Tin-Litho Toys*. Collectors Press: Portland, OR, 1995.

Kerr, Lisa and Jim Gilcher. *Ohio Art: The World of Toys*. Schiffer Publishing, Ltd.: Atglen, PA, 1998.

King, Constance Eileen. *The Encyclopedia of Toys*. Crown Publishers: New York, 1978.

Lantz, Louise K. *Old American Kitchenware: 1775 – 1925*. Thomas Nelson: New York, 1970.

Lechler, Doris. *Toy Glass.* Antique Publications: Marietta, OH, 1989.

L.H. Mace & Co. *Toys: Illustrated Catalogue and Net Price List.* L. H. Mace & Co.: New York, 1907; reprint, Washington Dolls' House & Toy Museum: Washington, D.C., 1977.

Long, Ernest and Ida. *Dictionary of Toys Sold in America.* 2 Vols. Ernest and Ida Long: Mokelumne Hill, CA, 1971 – 1978.

MacKay, James. *Childhood Antiques.* N.p.: Taplinger Publishing, 1976.

McClintock, Inez and Marshall. *Toys in America.* Public Affairs Press: Washington, D.C., 1961.

Needham, Walter. *A Book of Country Things.* Barrows Mussey, recorder. The Stephen Green Press: Brattleboro, VT, 1965.

O'Brien, Richard. *The Story of American Toys.* Abbeville Press: New York, 1990.

Panati, Charles. *Extraordinary Origin of Everyday Things.* Harper & Row Publishers: New York, 1987.

Phipps, Frances. *Colonial Kitchens, Their Furniture and Their Gardens.* Hawthorn Books, Inc.: New York, 1972.

Punchard, Lorraine. *Child's Play.* Lorraine Punchard: Bloomingdale, MN, 1982.

---. *Playtime Pottery and Porcelain.* Schiffer Publishing, Ltd.: Atglen, PA, 1996.

Roberts, Patricia Easterbrook. *Table Settings, Entertaining and Etiquette.* Viking Press: New York, 1967.

Schlereth, Thomas J. *Victorian America.* Harper Perennial: New York, 1992.

Schroeder, Joseph J. *Toys, Games & Dolls, 1860 – 1930.* DBI Books: Northfield, IL, 1971.

Shapiro, Laura. *Perfection Salad.* The Modern Library: New York, 2001.

Spero, James, ed. *Collectible Toys and Games of the Twenties and Thirties From Sears, Roebuck & Co. Catalogs.* Dover Publications, Inc.: New York, 1988.

Stille, Eva. *Doll Kitchens: 1800 – 1980.* Schiffer Publishing, Ltd.: West Chester, PA, 1988. Originally published in German, West Chester location given.

Stirn, Carl P. *Turn of the Century Dolls, Toys and Games: The Complete Illustrated Carl P. Stirn Catalog From 1893.* Henry Ford Museum & Greenfield Village: Dearborn, MI; Dover Publications, Inc.: New York, 1990.

Tunis, Edwin. *Colonial Craftsmen.* Johns Hopkins University Press: Baltimore, 1999.

White, Gwen. *Antique Toys and Their Background.* Arco: New York, 1971.

Whitmyer, Margaret and Kenn. *Children's Dishes.* Collector Books: Paducah, KY, 1984.

Whitton, Blair. *Toys.* Alfred A. Knopf: New York, 1984.

# Index

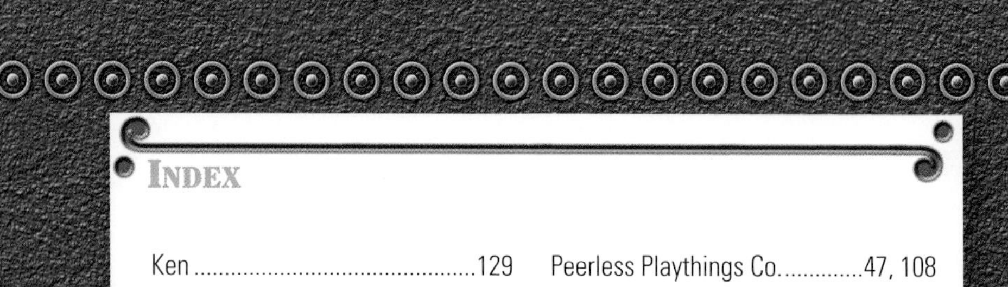

# more great TITLES from collector books

## DOLLS

2079 Barbie Doll Fashion, Volume I, Eames ........ $24.95
4846 Barbie Doll Fashion, Volume II, Eames ........ $24.95
6319 Barbie Doll Fashion, Volume III, Eames ........ $29.95
6546 Collector's Ency. of Barbie Doll Collector's Editions, Augustyniak ........ $29.95
6546 Collector's Ency. of Barbie Doll Exclusives & More, 3rd Ed., Augustyniak ........ $29.95
6451 Collector's Encyclopedia of American Composition Dolls, Volume II, Mertz ........ $29.95
6636 Collector's Encyclopedia of Madame Alexander Dolls, Crowsey ........ $24.95
5904 Collector's Guide to Celebrity Dolls, Spurgeon ........ $24.95
6456 Collector's Guide to Dolls of the 1960s and 1970s, Volume II, Sabulis ........ $24.95
6944 The Complete Guide to Shirley Temple Dolls and Collectibles, Bervaldi-Camaratta ........ $29.95
7028 Doll Values, Antique to Modern, 9th Edition, Edward ........ $14.95
6467 Paper Dolls of the 1960s, 1970s, and 1980s, Nichols ........ $24.95
6642 20th Century Paper Dolls, Young ........ $19.95

## TOYS & MARBLES

2333 Antique & Collectible Marbles, 3rd Edition, Grist ........ $9.95
6649 Big Book of Toy Airplanes, Miller ........ $24.95
6938 Everett Grist's Big Book of Marbles, 3rd Edition ........ $24.95
6466 Matchbox Toys, 1947 to 2003, 4th Edition, Johnson ........ $24.95
6840 Schroeder's Collectible Toys, Antique to Modern Price Guide, 10th Ed. ........ $17.95

## JEWELRY, WATCHES & PURSES

4850 Collectible Costume Jewelry, Simonds ........ $24.95
6468 Collector's Ency. of Pocket & Pendant Watches, 1500 – 1950, Bell ........ $24.95
6554 Coro Jewelry, Brown ........ $29.95
7025 Costume Jewelry 202, Carroll ........ $24.95
4940 Costume Jewelry, A Practical Handbook & Value Guide, Rezazadeh ........ $24.95
5812 Fifty Years of Collectible Fashion Jewelry, 1925 – 1975, Baker ........ $24.95
6833 Handkerchiefs: A Collector's Guide, Volume II, Guarnaccia/Guggenheim ........ $24.95
6464 Inside the Jewelry Box, Pitman ........ $24.95
5695 Ladies' Vintage Accessories, Johnson ........ $24.95
6645 100 Years of Purses, 1880s to 1980s, Aikins ........ $24.95
6942 Rhinestone Jewelry: Figurals, Animals, and Whimsicals, Brown ........ $24.95
6341 Signed Beauties of Costume Jewelry, Volume II, Brown ........ $24.95
6555 20th Century Costume Jewelry, Aikins ........ $24.95
5620 Unsigned Beauties of Costume Jewelry, Brown ........ $24.95
4878 Vintage & Contemporary Purse Accessories, Gerson ........ $24.95

1.800.626.5420 Mon. – Fri. 7am – 5 pm CT    Fax: 1.270.898.8890

## PAPER COLLECTIBLES & BOOKS

6623 Collecting **American Paintings**, James ....$29.95
6826 Collecting Vintage **Children's Greeting Cards**, McPherson ....$24.95
6553 Collector's Guide to **Cookbooks**, Daniels ....$24.95
6627 Early 20th Century **Hand-Painted Photography**, Ivankovich ....$24.95
6936 **Leather Bound Books**, Boutiette ....$24.95
6940 **Old Magazines**, 2nd Edition, Clear ....$19.95
6837 Vintage **Postcards** for the Holidays, 2nd Edition, Reed ....$24.95

## GLASSWARE

6821 Coll. **Glassware from the 40s, 50s & 60s**, 8th Edition, Florence ....$19.95
6830 Collector's Encyclopedia of **Depression Glass**, 17th Ed., Florence ....$19.95
3905 Collector's Encyclopedia of **Milk Glass**, Newbound ....$24.95
7029 **Elegant Glassware** of the Depression Era, 12th Edition, Florence ....$24.95
6334 Encyclopedia of **Paden City Glass**, Domitz ....$29.95
6126 **Fenton Art Glass**, 1907 – 1939, 2nd Ed., Whitmyer ....$29.95
6643 Florences' **Glassware Pattern Identification** Guide, Vol. IV ....$19.95
6641 Florences' **Ovenware** from the 1920s to the Present ....$24.95
6226 **Fostoria** Value Guide, Long/Seate ....$19.95
6461 The **Glass Candlestick** Book, Volume 3, Kanawha to Wright, Felt/Stoer ....$29.95
5827 **Kitchen Glassware** of the Depression Years, 6th Edition, Florence ....$24.95
6925 Standard Encyclopedia of **Carnival Glass**, 10th Ed., Edwards/Carwile ....$29.95
6476 **Westmoreland Glass**, The Popular Years, 1940 – 1985, Kovar ....$29.95

## OTHER COLLECTIBLES

6446 Antique & Contemporary **Advertising Memorabilia**, 2nd Edition, Summers ....$29.95
7024 B.J. Summers' Guide to **Coca-Cola**, 6th Edition ....$29.95
6625 Collector's Encyclopedia of **Bookends**, Kuritzky/De Costa ....$29.95
7042 The Ency. of Early American & Antique **Sewing Machines**, 3rd Ed., Bays ....$29.95
6932 **Flea Market Trader**, 15th Edition ....$12.95
6933 **Garage Sale** & Flea Market Annual, 14th Edition ....$19.95
7033 **Hot Kitchen** & Home Collectibles of the 30s, 40s, and 50s, Zweig ....$24.95
7040 **Schroeder's Antiques** Price Guide, 25th Edition ....$17.95
6038 **Sewing Tools** & Trinkets, Volume 2, Thompson ....$24.95
6841 Vintage **Fabrics**, Gridley/Kiplinger/McClure ....$19.95
6036 Vintage **Quilts**, Aug/Newman/Roy ....$24.95
6941 The Wonderful World of Collecting **Perfume Bottles**, Flanagan ....$29.95

This is only a partial listing of the books on antiques that are available from Collector Books. All books are well illustrated and contain current values. Most of these books are available from your local bookseller, antique dealer, or public library. If you are unable to locate certain titles in your area, you may order by mail from COLLECTOR BOOKS, P.O. Box 3009, Paducah, KY 42002-3009. Customers with Visa, MasterCard, or Discover may place orders by fax, by phone, or online. Add $4.00 postage for the first book ordered and 50¢ for each additional book. Include item number, title, and price when ordering. Allow 14 to 21 days for delivery.

cb

News for Collectors | Request a Catalog | Meet the Authors | Find Newest Releases | Calendar of Events | Special Sale Items

www.collectorbooks.com

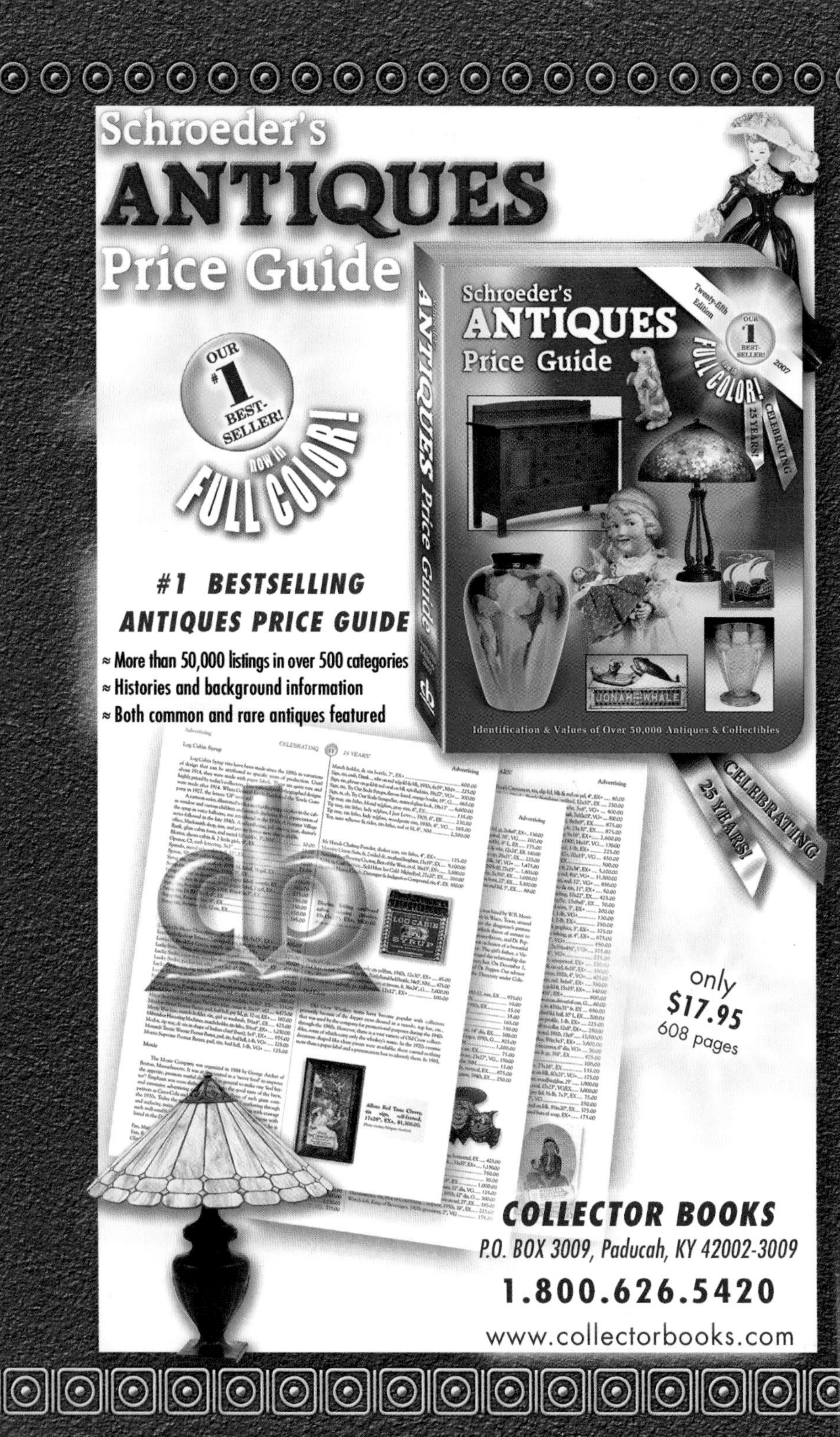

Schroeder's
ANTIQUES
Price Guide
OUR #1 BEST-SELLER!
now in FULL COLOR!
#1 BESTSELLING
ANTIQUES PRICE GUIDE
≈ More than 50,000 listings in over 500 categories
≈ Histories and background information
≈ Both common and rare antiques featured
CELEBRATING 25 YEARS!
only
$17.95
608 pages
COLLECTOR BOOKS
P.O. BOX 3009, Paducah, KY 42002-3009
1.800.626.5420
www.collectorbooks.com